Church of the Epiphany. St. Agnes guild

Par Excellence, a Manual of Cookery

Containing Choice Recipes

Church of the Epiphany. St. Agnes guild

Par Excellence, a Manual of Cookery
Containing Choice Recipes

ISBN/EAN: 9783744792516

Printed in Europe, USA, Canada, Australia, Japan

Cover: Foto ©Andreas Hilbeck / pixelio.de

More available books at **www.hansebooks.com**

PAR EXCELLENCE,

—A—

MANUAL OF COOKERY,

CONTAINING

CHOICE RECIPES,

contributed and
approved by the
best housekeepers
skilled in *cuisine,* the
whole carefully arranged and
compiled for St. Agnes Guild of the
Church of the Epiphany,
by a committee.

"She riseth while it is yet night and giveth meat to her household, and a portion to her maidens."

Proverbs 31-15.

CHICAGO:
PUBLISHED UNDER THE AUSPICES OF THE GUILD.
1888.

CONTENTS.

(SEE INDEX AT THE END.)

PREFACE.

Much of value that relates to modern *cuisine* lives not on the pages of cook books, but rather in recipes, directions and suggestions, passed oftentimes from mouth to mouth, hand to hand, penciled on some fly leaf, sent in a letter, pinned up here and pasted there. Of late much attention has been bestowed upon domestic cookery; costly and valuable treatises have always been in the market, and new ones on the subject are constantly appearing, but all these more or less lack the originality and force imparted by the skill and experience of the frugal housewife. The Guild has therefore sought to preserve the unwritten, legendary and traditional by obtaining, when possible, the original recipes from the most skillful and successful housekeepers, together with their suggestions and directions, added from experience. This publication has no pretension as a treatise, but is to be regarded rather as a sort of condiment, an appetizer, a delicacy in the art, so that by its use the action required of the housewife in preparing daily for the continual round of meals may not be confined to the cook-room, but legitimately transferred to the table — to the appetites of those that gather round it.

FOR THE GUILD BY THE COMMITTEE.

CHICAGO, Easter. 1888.

Tomato,	Mock Turtle,	Terrapin,
Ox Tail,	Okra or Gumbo,	Macaroni,
Pea,	Green Turtle,	Consommé,
Beet,	Julienne,	Soup and Bouilli,
Vermicelli,	Chicken,	Mullagatawny.

RICH and PERFECTLY SEASONED.

Require only to be heated, and are then ready to serve. | Prepared with great care from only the best materials. | Have enjoyed the highest reputation for more than 32 years.

TEST FREE

Send us 20 cents, to help pay express, and receive a sample can of Tomato Soup, prepaid, or your choice (excepting Green Turtle and Terrapin).

J. H. W. HUCKINS & CO.,

Sole Manufacturers, Boston, Mass.

SOLD BY ALL LEADING GROCERS.

SOUPS.

---

*"Noble deeds are held in honor
But this wide world sadly needs
Hearts of patience to unravel this—
The worth of common deeds."*

—*Anon.*

STOCK FOR SOUPS.

To every pound of meat and bone allow one quart of cold water, one even teaspoonful of salt, and half a saltspoon of pepper. Boil slowly but steadily, allowing one hour for each pound of meat. Skim carefully as often as any scum rises to the surface. Strain when done into a stone crock kept for the purpose, and when cold remove the cake of fat which will rise to the surface. If the stock is to be kept for several days leave the fat on until ready to use. Fresh and cooked meats may be used together. This stock will keep at least a week. Just before dinner each day it is only necessary to heat thoroughly, and by adding different flavorings and vegetables, you can have a new soup each day.

AMBER SOUP.

A large soup-bone boiled four hours with one chicken and small slice of ham. Then add one-half onion, one-half of a carrot, one piece celery, two pieces parsley, two summer savory, one thyme, three cloves, pepper and salt. Let it boil one hour longer and strain into earthen bowl to stand over night. Take off the fat and take out the jelly without disturbing the settlings. Add the well-beaten whites of two eggs and the shells. Boil one minute and skim well. Run the soup through a jelly bag. Color with burnt sugar and season with sherry wine when ready to serve.

BEAN SOUP.

Mrs. H. L. Hammond.

One pint of picked beans; wash and put on the fire with two quarts of cold water, a slice of salt pork, one very small red pepper, and a little salt. Boil two hours, or until beans are well cooked, strain through colander, and add milk or cream.

BEAN SOUP.

Mrs. Ryer.

Two pounds of salt pork, one quart of beans. Par-boil, and chop three onions. Boil slowly about six hours. Strain through a sieve. Serve with cubes of toast.

BEEF SOUP.

Any beef steak or roast beef that is left from previous meals can be used in this manner. Cut all the lean meat in small dice and roast them lightly in butter. Put in your saucepan two sliced onions, two carrots, half a turnip, half a pound of butter or the drippings from the roast or soup will do, let it all brown thoroughly, add one teacupful of floor and mix well. Have two and one-half quarts of stock boiling in the meantime, and add to the above, also adding one bay leaf, salt and pepper and a little celery, letting it all boil for two hours; during this time boil half a pound of barley well done in several waters, strain your soup, mix in the beef and the barley (off which the water

should be strained) allowing it to boil fifteen minutes, then season with a little Worcestershire sauce and sherry.

CARROT SOUP.

Cover the bones of any cold roast meat with two quarts of cold water; add one onion sliced and fried in butter, then one potatoe and one turnip, and six medium sized carrots, all pared and sliced. Simmer until the vegetables are tender, strain through a sieve, remove the bones and press the vegetables through. There should be about a quart and a pint. Put a spoonful of butter in a saucepan, stir in a spoonful of flour, and when smooth add the broth of puree, from which you have skimmed the fat. Season with salt and pepper, and add half a pint of hot cream. It should be as smooth as velvet and of the consistency of pea soup.

CELERY CREAM SOUP.

Mrs. H. H. Brown.

Add to a pint of milk, a tablespoonful of flour, one of butter, a head of celery, a large slice of onion and a small piece of mace. Boil celery in a pint of water from thirty to forty-five minutes; boil mace, onion and milk together. Mix flour with two tablespoonfuls of cold milk, and add to boiling milk. Add butter and season with salt and pepper to taste. Strain and serve immediately. This is improved by adding a cupful of whipped cream when soup is in tureen.

CELERY CREAM SOUP.

Mrs. C. S. McHenry.

One quart milk with a cup of cream, one teaspoonful of celery extract. Let cream and milk come almost to a boil, then add the extract, and thicken a little with flour and water. (In the meantime cut bread up in small pieces about the size of dice, and fry in butter to a nice brown.) Place the fried bread in a dish that it is to be served in and pour soup over it. Season *well*, but not until it is ready to serve. To be eaten as soon as ready.

CREAM OF CELERY.

Put one quart of veal stock into the saucepan, with six stalks of celery cut into half-inch pieces, one onion quartered, one blade of mace, a few whole peppers, salt. Boil one hour. Rub though a sieve and add one quart more of veal stock. Boil; then set on back of range to keep hot. Boil three pints of cream and strain into soup. Serve with small pieces of toast.

CLAM BROTH.

Chop up twenty-five small hard-shell clams. Then put them into a saucepan with their own liquor and a pint of water. Simmer fifteen minutes and strain. Add a dash of cayenne and a pea of butter. Just before serving add a gill of hot milk. Serve in thin tea or after-diner coffee cups. When the clams are purchased in the shell and home facilities for opening them are poor, wash them well. Cover them with hot water and let them cook until the shells open. When cool, remove the shells, chop the clams fine and if the water has not been made too salty, use it.

BISQUE OF CRABS.

Twelve hardshell crabs, one half pound butter, one teacupful of cold boiled rice, one heaping teaspoonful of salt, one soup bunch, one dozen whole peppers, three quarts of stock, yolk of one egg, one quart of warm boiled milk. Boil the crabs for one-half hour, then strain. When cold, break apart and pick out the meat. Put the under-shell and claws in the mortar, and pound as smooth as possible with the rice and butter. Put this in a saucepan and add the stock, herbs, salt and peppers. Boil slowly for one hour, pour through a sieve, working as much of the pulp through as possible. Keep the soup warm but not boiling, and add the milk with the beaten yolk slowly stirred into it. The milk should be warm. Season to taste.

Heat the crab meat in a little boiling water, drain, and put into a hot tureen and pour the soup in it. Serve.

CREAM SOUP.

Two quarts of good stock (beef or veal), one cup of sago, and one soup bunch. Boil well and season with pepper and salt. Strain carefully, and add one pint of cream.

CREAM OF CEREALINE.

Into two quarts of veal or chicken stock stir two cupfuls of "Cerealine;" boil for ten minutes; season with salt and pepper; rub through a sieve; return all to a soup kettle; add one cupful of milk, and bring it to a boil again; beat the yolks of two eggs very lightly, and put into a tureen; pour over them one cupful of boiling cream; stir well together, and follow with the hot soup, and serve with croutons of fried bread.

CREAM OF RICE.

Wash a half pound of rice, and put it into a saucepan with two quarts of stock. Boil slowly for an hour; then rub the rice through a sieve twice, return it to the stock. Salt and pepper to taste. Care must be taken that the rice does not stick to the bottom of the saucepan. Set on the back of stove until wanted. Beat up the yolk of two eggs; add them slowly to a quart of warm boiled milk. Pour the milk into the soup, which must not be too hot. Serve in hot tureen.

JULIENNE SOUP.

Time, one hour and a half. Three quarters of a pound of carrots, turnips, celery, onions, one large cabbage-lettuce, two ounces of butter, two lumps of sugar, five pints of clear soup, or medium stock.

Weigh three-quarters of a pound of the above named vegetables, and cut them into strips of about an inch and a half long, taking care they are all the same size; wash them in cold water, and drain them very dry; then put them into a stew-pan with the butter, and the sugar pounded. Set it over a quick fire for a few minutes, tossing them over frequently until they are covered with a thin glaze, but on no account allow the vegetables to burn; then add five pints of clear soup, or medium stock, cut the lettuce into pieces, and put it into the soup, and let it all stew gently for an hour or more.

GOOD FAMILY SOUP.

Take two pounds of coarse lean beef and half a pound of lean bacon in thin slices, and fry them with three slices of onions and a small fresh cabbage chopped. Put all into a stew-pan with two pounds of potatoes, three ounces of rice, two carrots, and one turnip, sliced, two teaspoonfuls of salt, and one of pepper. Pour over at first two quarts of water, and set the pan over a slow fire; skim carefully, and add by degrees two quarts more of water. Take out the potatoes when done, and mash them. After it has stewed three hours, take out the meat, and let the soup simmer another hour; then strain it and thicken it with the potatoes rubbed through a colander.

MULLACATAWNEY SOUP.

Brown an onion and turnip with a small slice of ham in a saucepan, mix in one cupful of flour, pour over it one-half gallon boiling stock, add two cans tomatoes and three large sour apples, cut up, and let it boil two hours, strain all through a fine sieve, cut in small pieces the meat of one-half a chicken, and add with one-half pound boiled rice to the above, season with two teaspoonfuls of curry powder, salt and pepper to taste.

NOODLE SOUP.

Break two eggs into a bowl; beat until light, adding a pinch of salt; then work in flour (with your hand) until you have a very stiff dough; turn it on your moulding board, and work until it is as smooth as glass; pinch off a piece the size of a

I. C. SILLIMAN,

FLORIST AND DECORATOR,

House Plants and Fresh Cut Flowers,

553 West Madison Street,

Telephone 7102. CHICAGO.

COOK & McLAIN,

CHICAGO STEAM DYE WORKS,

80 DEARBORN ST. & 261 W. MADISON ST.,

DYERS AND SCOURERS IN SILK AND WOOL.

Gentlemen's Garments Cleaned, Dyed, Repaired and Altered.

"CLEANFAST"

BLACK STOCKINGS,

POSITIVELY WILL NOT CROCK.

For Sale only by the

CLEANFAST HOSIERY CO.,

107 State Street, - - CHICAGO

Send for Price List.

TRY ONE PAIR AND BE CONVINCED.

ILLINOIS CENTRAL
R.R.
BETWEEN
CHICAGO
AND
ST. LOUIS
FREE FREE
RECLINING CHAIR CARS
ON · ALL · TRAINS.
FREE FREE
ELEGANT
PULLMAN
BUFFET SLEEPERS
ON
NIGHT TRAINS.
SEE THAT TICKETS READ
"VIA ILLINOIS CENTRAL R.R."

walnut, and roll it as thin as paper; then with a sharp knife cut off very narrow strips; proceed in the same way until all your dough is cut. Have prepared some good veal, chicken, or any other kind of broth, well seasoned, one-half an hour before you serve dinner, drop in the noodles. Be sure the soup is boiling. Add a little parsley. If the noodles are made according to directions they will be found far superior to macaroni.

OYSTER PLANT SOUP.

Mrs. Graeme Stuart.

To one quart of milk take three bunches of oyster plant, scrape and clean, cut into pieces of half an inch thickness, and let stand in salt water fifteen minutes. Put on to boil with enough water to cover. When tender, have ready one quart of milk (do not turn the water off), a piece of butter, pepper and salt to taste, and let come to a boil; use cracker meal to thicken, if preferred.

PEA SOUP WITHOUT MEAT.

Time, three hours. One pint of split peas, three quarts of water, six large onions, outside sticks of two heads of celery, one bunch of sweet herbs, two carrots, a little dried mint, a handful of spinach, a few bones, or tiny pieces of bacon flavor it nicely; pepper and salt to your taste.

Boil all these vegetables together till they are quite soft and tender, strain them through a hair sieve, pressing the carrot pulp through it. Then boil the soup well for an hour with the best part of the celery, and a teaspoonful of pepper, add a little dried mint and fried bread, with a little spinach. A few roast-beef bones, or a slice of bacon, will be an improvement.

SPLIT PEA SOUP.

Cut two slices of ham and one onion into small pieces and fry until slightly brown, in a little bacon fat. Cut up one turnip, one carrot and four stalks of celery and add to the ham and onion, letting them simmer for fifteen minutes, then pour over them three quarts of hot water, and add a pint of split peas, which have been soaked over night in cold water. Boil gently until the peas are quite tender, stirring constantly to prevent burning, then add one teaspoonful of brown sugar ; salt and pepper to taste. Rub through a sieve ; return to the fire and let it simmer for half an hour. Pour into a hot tureen and serve with fried bread cut into dice.

POTATO SOUP.

Mrs. H. H. Brown.

A quart of milk, six large potatoes, one stalk of celery, an onion and a tablespoonful of butter. Put the milk to boil with onion and celery. Pare potatoes and boil thirty minutes. Turn off the water, mash fine and light. Add boiling milk and the butter, and pepper and salt to taste. Rub through strainer and serve immediately. A cupful of whipped cream added when in the tureen is a great improvement. This soup must not be allowed to stand, not even if kept hot. Serve immediately and it is excellent.

POTATO SOUP.

Boil one quart of milk, when boiling stir in four large potatoes, boiled and mashed fine. Boil together a few minutes. Season with butter, pepper and salt. Put a well-beaten egg in the tureen and into it strain soup.

RICH BRCWN CRAVY SOUP.

Take four pounds of beef steak, quite lean, and fry it a light brown with three sliced onions; put into a stewpan four ounces of butte r, and when dissolved, shake it round the pan, and lay in the meat and onions with a carrot, a turnip, and a head of celery sliced, a blade of mace, two teaspoonsful of salt, and a little cayenne pepper. Pour over a quart of clear stock, and stew gently, adding by degrees two quarts of water, and carefully removing the scum as it rises. Let it simmer for six hours, then strain, and, when cool, clear it of the fat. When heated, add a glass of Madeira or sherry. This is a strong and rich soup. Serve with boiled macaroni cut in pieces in it.

TOMATO CREAM SOUP.

Mrs. Graeme Stuart.

To one can tomatoes, stewed and strained, take one quart of sweet milk, and let come to a boil, and before putting in tomatoes, put a pinch of soda in them, so as not to curdle the milk, season with salt, pepper, and a piece of butter, and a little flour to thicken. Serve with fried bread cut in small pieces.

TOMATO SOUP.

Mrs. H. H. Brown.

One quart can tomatoes, two heaping tablespoonsful of flour, one of butter, one teaspoonful of salt, one of sugar, and a pint of hot water. Let tomatoes and water come to a boil. Put flour, butter, and a tablespoonful of tomatoes together. Stir into boiling mixture, add seasoning, boil altogether fifteen minutes, rub through a sieve, and serve with toasted bread. This bread should first be cut in thin slices; should be buttered, cut into little squares, placed in a pan buttered side up, and browned in a quick oven.

TOMATO SOUP.

Mrs. Babcock, Cleveland.

Proportion: To one cup of tomatoes add one cup of water, one cup of milk, one soda cracker rolled, pepper, salt and butter, soda the size of a pea put in with the tomatoes to prevent curdling the milk.

TOMATO SOUP.

Mrs. W. A. Hammond.

Three pints beef stock, one half can tomatoes, three good sized potatoes cut up fine, one soup bunch, pepper and salt to taste. Strain through colander before sending to the table.

LOBSTER SOUP.

Mrs. A. D. Smith.

Wash and boil shells two or three hours, after picking out the meat, strain stock and add as much cream and milk as there is broth. Roll two small crackers and put in, season with cayenne pepper and salt. After simmering a few moments add meat of lobster picked very fine and two tablespoons of butter.

TOMATO SOUP.

Two quarts of tomatoes, peeled and sliced, add three pints of broth—veal or chicken is best; one tablespoonful minced parsley, and the same quantity of minced onion, one teaspoonful of sugar; pepper and salt to taste; browned flour for thickening; tablespoonful of butter, fried bread dice. Stew the tomatoes in the broth until they are broken all to pieces, add herbs and onion; stew twenty minutes, rub through a colander, season, thicken with a tablespoonful of browned flour, rubbed in one of butter; boil two minutes, and pour upon fried bread in the tureen.

GREEN TURTLE SOUP.

To make this soup canned turtle is generally used, unless you can get prepared turtle from your caterer, which is by far the best. One can of green turtle will make one gallon of soup. Cut the meat in dice pieces, add a little stock, and let it simmer for ten minutes in this liquor, put the vegetables sliced with one pound of butter, two slices of ham and a small veal bone in your pot, and let it all brown thoroughly, mixing a cup of flour after browning. Pour on this one gallon boiling stock, add celery, a few tomatoes whole peppers and allspice, and let it boil three hours, adding enough stock to keep the amount of soup wanted, strain and season to taste; add one cupful of sherry, half a cup of madeira, and the juice of a lemon, mix in your turtle, and the soup is ready to serve.

MOCK TURTLE SOUP.

Prepare your soup in the same manner as for green turtle, and when strained add meat off from a calf's foot cut into dice shape pieces, also add a few quenelles prepared in following manner: Rub the yolks of two hard boiled eggs very fine, add the yolks of two raw eggs and one whole egg, season with salt, pepper and a little nutmeg, stiffen to a dough with flour, roll

The Arnold Automatic Steam Cooker

Is Unequaled for Cooking Anything that Can Be Boiled, Baked or Roasted.

It is constructed so that the Most Effective Results are obtained for the Least Amount of Fuel, Time and Trouble. It can be used on any kind of stove—Coal, Wood, Oil or Gas.

ADVANTAGES.

A whole dinner can be put in *at once*, covered up, and *let alone* until ready to serve.

A poor cook cannot spoil the meal if she tries.

A good cook can cook better with one than without it.

The ordinary heat of a cooking stove, or a gas, gasoline or oil flame, will generate steam in three minutes.

No steam or odor escapes into the room.

The meal may be kept for hours.

Everything cooked in it is healthier and more easily digested than when cooked by any other method.

It saves nearly one-third of the food that is lost by the ordinary methods.

All the nutriment, richness and flavor of the food is retained.

It saves the labor of watching.

Burning, scorching, smoking or over-cooking is impossible.

It never boils over.

The ARNOLD COOKER, which I use in my public lectures, as well as in my home, is certainly one of the important improvements in cookery. Experience enables me to give it the highest praise.

DR. BEARDSLEY, N. Y.

From the Principal of the Philadelphia Cooking School.—I have examined for the Franklin Institute the ARNOLD AUTOMATIC STEAM COOKER, and I think it superior in every respect to other steamers.

S. T. RORER.

CHICAGO, Feb. 24, 1888.—After 18 months' experience with the ARNOLD COOKER, will say that if cooks knew its merits they would have one. ALEXANDER TESTAULT, Butler for George M. Pullman.

CHICAGO, Feb. 24, 1888.—We have used the AUTOMATIC STEAM COOKER constantly for more than three years. It is simply indispensable.

MRS. H. B. MOSS,
MRS. M. A. MITCHELL,
MRS. C. B. SAWYER,
MRS. A. W. SIMPSON.

CHICAGO, May 11, 1887.—To HOUSEKEEPERS: Ladies, it gives me pleasure to subscribe words of praise to the capital workings of the ARNOLD STEAM COOKER.

MRS. CHAS. SPRINGER,
MRS. O. C. WIEDNER,
MRS. G. J. SMITH,
MRS. GEO. ROPE.

Each Cooker is accompanied by Explicit Directions, Valuable Recipes, and Dr. B. F. Beardsley's Great Lecture, "What to Eat and How to Eat It."

Our Agent will call and show you the Cooker, or we will mail you a circular with full information.

SOLD BY AUTHORIZED AGENTS ONLY.

Address R. C. OWENS, 118 18th St., Agent for Chicago.

into little balls, the size of a large pea, boil in water twenty minutes, strain and mix in soup, use the same wine and a little Worcestershire sauce as for green turtle soup.

VEAL SOUP.

Mrs. W. A. Hammond.

Two quarts good veal stock, one bunch celery, one teacup spaghuetti broken in pieces about an inch long. Cook spaghuetti in one quart of water until tender; into this strain the stock and add one bunch of celery. When it has boiled about five minutes take out the celery; add one teacup of cream, and season to taste. If you have no cream use milk and one tablespoonful butter.

VEGETABLE SOUP.

Time, four hours and a half. Three onions, six potatoes, six carrots, four turnips, half a pound of butter, four quarts of water, one head of celery, a spoonful of catsup, a bunch of sweet herbs. Peel, slice and fry the vegetables, etc., in half a pound of butter, and pour over them two quarts of boiling water; let them stew slowly for four hours, then strain through a coarse cloth or sieve; put the soup into the stewpan with the head of celery. Stew till tender.

FRANK PYATT,

PHARMACIST,

438 W. MADISON ST., CHICAGO, ILL.,

Prescriptions Accurately Compounded

At all Hours Day or Night.

DRUGS, CHEMICALS AND PATENT MEDICINES, ETC.

ALL LADIES SHOULD USE

BATES' FRIZZETTA

As it is the only article that will successfully keep the hair in curl in the warmest assembly or ball room, or in the dampest of weather. Mr. Pyatt is Sole Agent for the United States for this article.

We will also respectfully call your attention to an article called

CURDEM,

Manufactured by Mr. Pyatt, for Chapped Face and Hands, Tan, Sunburn, Freckles, etc. It cannot be excelled. Sold by druggists generally, at twenty-five cents per bottle.

FISH.

PICKING OUT FISH.

Salmon, pike, bluefish, whitefish, trout, carp, trench, grayling, carbel, chub, ruff, eel, whiting, smelt, shad, pickerel, etc., are known to be fresh or stale by the smell and color of their gills, the hanging or keeping up of the fins, and the standing out or sinking of the eyes. If sturgeon cuts without crumbling, the veins and gristles are a genuine blue and the flesh perfectly white, it is good. Cod and codling can be chosen by the thickness near the head and whiteness of the flesh when cut. Turbot should be chosen by the thickness and plumpness; if the flesh be thick and the belly of a cream color it will be palatable; if otherwise, it is not good. The gills of herring and mackerel should be of a bright red, the eyes full and the fish stiff; when dusky and faded, and the tails very pliable, they are stale. The best lobsters are the heaviest if there is no water in them; if fresh the tail will be full of hard or red-skinned meat. A cock lobster is known by narrow back part of the tail, and the two uppermost fins within his tail are stiff and hard; the hen is soft and the back of her tail broader. If the flesh of pickled salmon feels oily and the scales stiff and shining, and it comes in flakes and parts without crumbling, it is fresh and good, but not otherwise.

BAKED FISH.

Scale, wash and wipe dry, inside and out, a 2 or 3 pound fish. Make a stuffing as follows: One pint grated bread; two tablespoonfuls melted butter, pepper and salt to taste, one raw egg, a little celery salt, one onion chopped fine, is, to my taste, an improvement, but can be omitted, if not liked. Care should be taken not to wet the bread-crumbs; the egg and melted butter will moisten sufficiently. Tie over the fish thin slices of salt pork, fill a dripping pan half full of hot water, then, if you have not a wire grate, place the gridiron on the pan, and after laying the fish on the gridiron cover all with another pan, bake in a hot oven till the pork is well shrivelled, then remove the upper tin, allowing your fish to brown. One and a half hours will cook thoroughly, if a steady fire is kept.

BAKED BLUE FISH.

Split the fish open, remove the bone, and lay it in pan, skin next to pan, which should be buttered beforehand, season with salt and pepper, sprinkle over the fish melted butter, and put in oven to bake, in the meantime strain the contents of a tomato can, and mix with a little cracker crumbs, season with salt, pepper, a little Worcestershire sauce and ground mace, pour this over the fish when half done, just enough to cover lightly, and bake to a finish, the rest of the sauce may be kept hot and sent to the table with fish. All fish baked in this manner will prove very delicious.

BOILED FISH.

Delmonico's Method.

From a reliable source, the following is presented as Delmonico's method for boiling fish: The fish should be washed as little as possible, and whitefish, after being cleaned and wiped with a damp cloth, should have the stomach stuffed with salt for an hour or two before cooking. Fish should be put on in cold water, so that the inner part may be sufficiently done, and it is also less liable to break. This rule holds good, except for very small fish, or for salmon boiled in slices, when boiling water should be used. The time may be easily known when it is ready by drawing up the fish-plate and trying if it will separate from the bone. A little salt and vinegar should

always be put into the water. Some prefer their fish boiled in what is called a court bouillon, and this is how it is done: Lay the fish in the kettle with enough cold water to cover it, add a glass of wine or vinegar, some sliced carrot and onions, pepper, salt and a laurel leaf, a bunch of parsley, a fagot of sweet herbs, or some of the same tied up in a muslin bag. These seasonings impart a fine flavor to most boiled fish, excepting salmon, and for fresh-water fish it is considered very useful for getting rid of the muddy taste they often have.

SALT CODFISH IN CREAM.

Pick the fish very fine and let it soak for four hours, wash off this water and let it soak for one hour in boiling water, do not boil, put in a saucepan one-half cup good butter, when melted stir in one-halfcupful of flour and then one pint of boiling milk, let it come to a boil and strain; strain your codfish very dry and mix in the above sauce, when it is ready to serve.

ESCALLOPED FISH.

Mrs. Graeme Stewart.

Boil a white fish; when cool, pick into small pieces, and butter some shells, or individual dishes. A layer of fish, then cracker meal, season with bits of butter, salt and pepper, and so on, till the dish is full. Have ready one-half pint cream, and same quantity of milk, with an egg beaten into it, pour over the fish just as much as possible, so that the fish will be very moist when done, Put the shells in a dripping pan with a little water in the bottom, so as not to burn, and brown nicely for fifteen minutes. Serve with drawn butter sauce, flavored with Worcestershire, or chopped parsley, as desired.

FISH BALLS.

Mrs. Babcock, Cleveland.

One and a half cups of fish after it is prepared, three cups of potatoes mashed, whites of two eggs beaten to a stiff froth. Mix and fry as doughnuts.

FISH BALLS NO. 2.

Mrs. E. J. Hill.

One and a half cups of fish, two cups mashed potatoes, one egg, a small piece of butter (about a tablespoonful), and a small quantity of black pepper, mix well and fry in a spider with plenty of sweet lard.

CODFISH CAKES.

One pint of codfish picked up fine, one quart of potatoes, two eggs, three tablespoonsful milk, a little pepper, and butter the size of an egg. Put the pared potatoes in a kettle, turn codfish over them, cover well with cold water. Boil till potatoes are cooked. Then drain through a colander, mash fine; put in the butter, pepper and milk. Beat well—the longer the better. Then add eggs well beaten. Have fat hot, as you would have for fried cakes. Drop it into the lard by the spoonful and fry until brown. To bake this codfish, grease a tin, put the codfish into it and bake until brown; then turn it out on a platter to serve with drawn butter over it.

FISH BALLS.

One pint of finely chopped cooked salt fish, six medium-sized potatoes, one egg, one heaping tablespoonful of butter, pepper, two tablespoonfuls of cream, or four of milk. Pare the potatoes, and put on in boiling water. Boil half an hour. Drain off all the water, turn the potatoes into the tray with the fish, mash fine and light with vegetable masher. Add the butter, pepper, milk and eggs, and mix all thoroughly. Taste to see if salt enough. Shape into balls the size of an egg and fry brown in boiling fat enough to float them. They will cook in three minutes and be a beautiful brown if the fat is smoking hot.

FRESH MACKEREL BROILED.

Split the fish open, remove the backbone and broil over a quick fire, basting it freely with butter, season with salt and pepper, and serve it with parsley butter, and slice of lemon.

SALT MACKEREL.

These fish should be soaked in fresh cold water for twenty-four hours, when they are ready for use.

BROILED SALT MACKEREL.

Handle in the same manner as a fresh mackerel, only leave out salt and pepper and parsley butter, baste with butter while broiling.

SALT MACKEREL BOILED.

Boil about ten minutes and serve with melted butter poured on them.

BOILED SALMON.

Time, according to weight. One salmon, four ounces of salt to one gallon of water.

Salmon is put into warm water instead of cold, in order to preserve its color and set the curd. It should be thoroughly well dressed to be wholesome.

Scale it, empty and wash it with the greatest care. Do not leave any blood on the inside that you can remove.

Boil the salt rapidly in the fishkettle for a minute or two, taking off the scum as it rises; put in the salmon, and let it boil gently till it is thoroughly done. Take it from the water on the fishplate, let it drain, put it on a hot folded fish-napkin, and garnish with slices of lemon. Sauce: shrimp or lobster.

Send up dressed cucumber with salmon when in season.

MIDDLE SLICE OF SALMON.

Time, ten minutes to the pound. Middle piece or slice.

Boil slowly in salt and water. Salmon should be put into warm water, which makes it eat firmer. Boil gently. Serve on a napkin. Sauce: lobster, shrimp, or plain melted butter and parsley.

BROILED SALMON.

Time, ten to fifteen minutes. Slices from the middle of a salmon, one tablespoonful of flour, a sheet or two of oiled letter paper, a little cayenne pepper.

Cut slices of an inch or an inch and a half thick from the middle of a large salmon; dust a little cayenne pepper over them, wrap them in oiled or buttered paper, broil them over a clear fire, first rubbing the bars of the gridiron with suet.

Broiled salmon is extremely rich and really requires no sauce; nevertheless, one especially intended for it will be found among the list of sauces.

The slices may also be simply dried in a cloth, floured and boiled over a clear fire; but they require the *greatest* care then to prevent them from burning. The gridiron is always rubbed with suet first.

Fresh, boiled salmon cold is a delicious fish course for a hot summer's day dinner. Great care must be taken in the boiling to keep the fish whole. When done it must be placed on the ice for two or three hours to insure its being not only cold, but very firm. Serve with a mayonnaise dressing in which there is a good deal of lemon juice or vinegar.

BAKED SMELTS.

Mrs. Dr. Leroy.

Smelts should be seasoned well with salt and pepper, dipped in butter, then in flour, and baked ten minutes in a very hot oven. Serve on buttered soft toast.

FRIED SMELTS.

Open the smelts at the head, draw, wash, and wipe dry, roll in flour, dip in egg beaten with a little milk, season with salt and pepper, then roll in cracker crumbs and fry brown in hot lard.

FISH TURBOT.

Mrs. H. H. Brown.

Boil five or six pounds of haddock or whitefish. Take out all bones, and shred fish fine. Let a quart of milk, a quarter of an onion, and a piece of parsley come to a boil, then stir in a scant cupful of flour, which has been mixed with a cup of cold milk and the yolks of two eggs. Season with half a teaspoonful of white pepper, the same quantity of thyme, half a cupful of butter, and well with salt. Butter a pan, and put in first a layer of sauce, then one of fish. Finish with sauce, and over it sprinkle cracker crumbs and a light grating of cheese. Bake an hour in a moderate oven. This quantity can of course be divided.

OYSTERS.

BROILED OYSTERS.

Select nice, fresh, large oysters, drain and have them dry, dip one by one into melted butter, and place them in a wire gridiron, broil over a clear fire. When brown on both sides, add salt and pepper and baste with plenty of good butter; serve on toast dipped in hot water and buttered. They must be served hot to be relished; they are also nice to be served on top of steaks.

CREAMED OYSTERS.

Mrs. H. H. Brown.

A pint of cream, one quart of oysters, a small piece of onion, a very small piece of mace, a tablespoonful of flour, and salt and pepper to taste. Let cream, with the onion and mace, come to a boil. Mix flour with cold milk and stir in boiling cream. Let oysters come to a boil in their own liquor; skim carefully. Drain off all the liquor and turn the oysters into the cream. Skim out mace and onion and serve.

ESCALOPED OYSTERS.

Mrs. H H. Brown.

Two quarts of oysters, half-cupful of butter, half-cupful of cream or milk, four teaspoonfuls of salt, half a teaspoonful of pepper, two quarts of stale bread crumbs. Butter the escalop dishes and put in a layer of crumbs and then one of oysters. Dredge with salt and pepper, and put small pieces of butter here and there in the dish. Now have another layer of oysters, seasoning as before, then add milk, and, finally a thick layer of crumbs, which dot with butter. Bake twenty minutes in quick oven. The crumbs must be light and flakey. The quantity given is enough for two dishes.

ESCALOPED OYSTERS.

Mrs. C. S. McHenry.

One quart oysters, one quart cracker crumbs, one coffee cup melted butter, thoroughly mixed through the crackers. Butter a deep baking dish, cover the bottom with the crumbs, put in a layer of oysters, seasoned well with pepper, salt and bits of butter, then a layer of crumbs, then oysters, and so on until the dish is full, and pour over the whole one large coffee cup of cream and bake three-fourths of an hour. (Excellent.)

LITTLE PIGS IN BLANKETS.

Select large sized oysters. Cut English breakfast bacon in thin smooth slices; wrap an oyster in each, fastening with a wooden toothpick. Season oysters with salt and pepper. Have frying pan hot, and let them cook long enough to crisp the bacon but not to burn. This is a nice dish for luncheon.

FRIED OYSTERS.

Roll in cracker crumbs and fry in equal quantities of butter and lard; use large oysters; pepper and salt to taste.

FRIED OYSTERS, NO. 2.

Roll in corn meal and fry in hot lard. Serve on a napkin.

OYSTER PATTIES.

Line a deep pie plate or patty pan with a crust, fill with a fricassee of oysters, cover with a thin layer of good puff paste, and bake in hot oven.

FILLING FOR OYSTER PATTIES.

Take two ounces butter, one-half pint sweet cream, pepper and salt, three tablespoonfuls flour, three dozen count oysters. Melt the butter, stir in the flour, boil the cream, and stir it in, cook the oysters in their own broth, till they are just cooked through, skim off the broth and add to the cream sauce, and fill the crust.

DELMONICO'S STEWS.

The following is the formula used at the celebrated restaurants of Delmonico in New York, where, it is said, the finest oyster stews in the world are obtainable :

Take one quart of liquid oysters, put the liquor (a teacupful for three persons) in a stewpan, and add one-half as much more water; salt, a good bit of pepper, a teaspoonful of butter for each person, and a teaspoonful of rolled cracker for each. Put on the stove and let it boil; have the oysters ready in a bowl. The moment the liquor begins to boil pour in all the oysters, say ten for each person. Now watch carefully, and as soon as it begins to boil count just thirty seconds, and take the oysters from the stove. Have a big dish ready with one and one-half tablespoonfuls of cold milk for each person. Pour the stew on this milk and serve immediately. Never boil an oyster if you wish it to be good.

PICKLED OYSTERS.

One-half ounce each of allspice, mace, cinnamon, cloves, one-half quart of vinegar, scald all together, then put in your oysters, let it cool, next day scald all together again, and let cool for use.

MEATS.

"We are shaped and fashioned by what we love."—Goethe.

In roasting beef allow about twelve minutes to a pound; for mutton about fifteen minutes to a pound.

For broiling always grease the griddle well and have it very hot before putting on the meat. It is well to cover the meat while cooking. Frying means cooking by immersion in hot lard, butter or oil—not, as is generally understood by this term: cooking in a spoonful of fat, first on one side then on the other. If the fat is hot enough, a brown crust is instantly formed on the outside of the article immersed, thereby keeping the inside perfectly free from grease.

Poultry should never be eaten less than six or eight hours after it is killed, but should be picked and drawn as soon as possible.

ROAST BEEF.

A three rib roast weighing ten pounds should be roasted one and one-half hours in hot oven, so as to have rare. Put in pan one sliced onion and one carrot, place your roast on top of vegetables, salt it, put some fat skimmed off soups in pan, and put in oven. When vegetables and meat are brown add one pint hot water; do not turn the meat too often but baste frequently. If the sauce gets too low in pan add a little warm water, when the meat is done strain off the sauce, skim off all fat, season with salt and pepper and serve.

BEEF A LA MODE.

Buy a good roast—the tenderloin. Have the butcher put in a good piece of fat before he skewers it. Put in your ham boiler, or a kettle that can be hermetically (air tight) closed, an inch-thick slice of salt pork cut in small pieces, a pound of veal, a piece of butter, some salt, two or three cloves, some whole pepper, one onion cut in quarters, and one carrot quartered lengthwise. Lay the roast in, pour over a spoonful of vinegar, close and set over the fire, not too hot. In about ten minutes add a cup of water, and turn the meat, in fifteen, another cup, and in twenty more, another. Turn occasionally, but keep closed. Simmer slowly four hours. When done, carefully place upon a platter, putting a piece of carrot on each side, top and bottom. Turn all the grease out of the kettle, pour two tablespoonfuls of water into the kettle, give another boil, and turn over the meat.

BEEF STEW.

In a stewpan place a large tablespoonful of butter, in which fry until quite brown two sliced onions, adding while cooking twelve whole cloves, ditto, allspice, one-half a teaspoonful of salt, and one-half that quantity of black pepper. Take from fire, pour in a pint of cold water, wherein lay two or three pounds of tender, lean beef cut in small, thick pieces. Cover closely, and let all stew gently two hours, adding just before serving a little flour thickening. A few sprigs of sweet basil is an improvement.

BEEFSTEAK BROILED.

Butter your steak and broil quickly over a clear fire, season with salt and pepper, put piece of good butter on plate and the steak on top and serve at once.

CORNED BEEF.

This meat should be boiled slow and when done take pot and all from the fire, leaving the corned beef in its stock until wanted to send to table. Any piece left over to be used as cold, should be put in this stock and left there until thoroughly cold, then put on plate in refrigerator.

CORNED BEEF HASH.

Take cold lean corned beef and chop very fine, chop cold boiled potatoes, and take, of these half and half, mix with a little stock and season with a little salt and pepper; sometimes the corned beef is salty enough to omit the salt, and bake in oven or fry in pan like small omelets.

TO PICKLE BEEF, HAMS, ETC.

Mrs. Hammond.

To four gallons of water add one and one-half pounds sugar, or one pint of molasses, two ounces of saltpetre, and nine pounds salt. Put the whole into a pot and let it boil, being careful to take off the scum as it rises. Then take it off to cool, after which cover the meat with it once in two minutes, boil the pickle, taking off the scum and adding two ounces of sugar, and one and one-half pounds of salt. The pickle will hold good for twelve months and is incomparable for ham, tongues and beef.

BAKED HAM.

Make a crust of water and flour, roll half an inch thick, soak your ham over night and scrape well, then cover nice and tight with the crust, so the juice cannot escape, and bake it till done. Then remove all the crust and serve.

BOILED HAM.

Clean thoroughly before cutting for any purpose. To boil, put in kettle of *cold water*, boil slowly till tender, and, if intended to be eaten when cold, let it remain in the kettle just as it was cooked until cold.

ESCALOPED HAM.

Chop cold boiled ham until very fine. Scald one pint of milk and stir into it. Remove from the fire, and add one well beaten egg and pour into a well buttered dish. Strew a thick layer of cracker crumbs over the top, and put in pieces of butter as for escaloped oysters. Season with a little cayenne pepper. Bake.

NEW ENGLAND BOILED DINNER.

Boil one piece of corned beef, brisket part if you can get it, and a piece of lean salt pork, boil two large carrots, a sweet turnip, two heads cabbage, two beets, a few onions and potatoes. Serve the meat and vegetables sliced. Beets should be cooked separately, also the onions and potatoes, but cook all vegetables, with exception of the beets, in some of the corned beef stock, to give them seasoning and flavor.

STEWED KIDNEY.

Cut the kidneys into small pieces. Wash thoroughly. Let them boil until tender; add to the water in which they are boiled; butter, pepper and salt, to taste. Stir a little flour in cold water, and add to thicken the gravy. This may be poured over buttered toast.

ROAST LEG OF LAMB.

Time, one hour and three-quarters for six pounds. When cooked, remove the lamb and thicken contents of the dripping pan with flour. Serve with mint sauce and a salad.

LAMB ROAST, MINT SAUCE.

Roast one-quarter lamb, in hot oven, for about forty-five minutes. Prepare with sauce, to be served with lamb as follows: Chop one bunch of mint very fine, rub together with a cupful of fine sugar, dissolve in one pint wine vinegar, and keep cold. There are some cooks who will boil the mint sauce. Strain and serve either hot or cold.

BOILED LEG OF MUTTON, CAPER SAUCE.

Boil a leg of mutton slowly for several hours in salted water. Boil a few whole turnips with it and serve as a vegetable. Serve caper sauce as per recipe.

Caper Sauce.—Mix in a pint of allemande sauce, one cupful of capers and serve.

WHITE SAUCE OR ALLEMANDE.

Put in a sauce pan a cupful of butter, a sliced onion and carrot. When melted add a cupful of flour, stir in three quarts boiling white stock and let it boil one hour, season with salt and white pepper, strain, beat the yolks of two eggs with the juice of a lemon and stir into this sauce and keep hot for use.

BAKED MEAT PIE.

Take cold meat and chop finely; then take alternate layers of the meat and sliced or stewed tomatoes. Put in a buttered dish; season with salt, pepper and lumps of butter, and one small onion chopped. Thicken with a handful of flour, cover with a rich crust and bake one hour.

HASHED LAMB ON TOAST WITH POACHED EGG.

Any pieces of cold lamb, left over from a dinner, can be use for the above dish. Chop the lamb very fine, boil two potatoes, mash fine, add the lamb and enough Allemande sauce to make it the consistency of hash, season with salt, pepper and a little ground mace, have it hot. Serve on toast with a poached egg on top.

PORK TENDERLOIN.

Cut the tenderloin open; stew in water till nearly done, then with a little butter hissing in a spider, fry to a light, brown—not too hard; have a small piece of toast buttered for each piece of meat; place the meat on the toast, pepper and salt and then throw a thin milk gravy over all. We call it "quail on toast," and think it a very good substitute.

PORK CHOPS.

Trim and dip in beaten egg, then in cracker crumbs seasoned with salt, pepper, onion and sage. Fry in hot lard twenty minutes, turning often.

SCOTCH STEW.

Mrs. H. J. Jones.

Three pounds of lean beef passed through a sausage cutter, taking out all fat and skin, etc., one small onion chopped fine, salt and pepper to taste. Put in a deep vessel, with one cup boiling water, cover and stew slowly three hours, then add a large spoonful of butter.

LAMB CHOPS SAUTE, WITH PEAS.

Trim about 12 lbs lamb chops, neat and evenly, place in frying pan with a little butter, and fry to a brown color, season with salt and pepper and when done, place the chops on a dish in a circle, having between each chop a nicely browned piece of toast, strain the sugar off a can French peas, put the peas in pan with a piece of butter, salt and pepper, toast them until hot, put in middle of plate, the lamb chops around them.

ROULADE OF SPRING LAMB.

Obtain the loin of a lamb, bone it, roll and tie together. Roast the same in a hot oven for about fifteen or twenty minutes. Serve the lamb on plate, garnish with milk sauce, and serve.

PIGS' FEET.

Mrs. H. H. Jones.

Take the feet that have not been pickled, boil them till perfectly done, when cold, split, and roll in a thin batter of milk, egg and flour, and fry quickly in hot lard, and you will have a delicious breakfast or lunch dish.

BROILED TRIPE.

Cut the tripe in large, square pieces, baste with butter and broil over a quick fire. Season with salt and pepper, using butter freely to keep the tripe soft.

FRIED TRIPE.

Cut into squares, dip in corn meal, fry in hot lard to a nice brown. Put a small bit of butter on each piece and serve.

TO COOK TONGUE.

French receipt for cooking tongue: After boiling it as usual, until tender, cut into small pieces, and brown with flour and butter. Then add some of the stock, season highly, let it boil a few moments and serve hot.

VEAL CUTLETS.

A nice way to cook cutlets and chops is to bake them. The great object is to have veal and mutton thoroughly cooked, and by baking you best accomplish that object. Take your

dripping-pan, rub a little butter over each cutlet, salt and pepper and lay flat in pans, place in hot oven, and cover with another pan of same size. When done, if you like, make a sauce called butter *maitre d'hotel.* Rub to a soft paste a small piece of butter with flour, pour over half a cup boiling hot water. It will then thicken, then add a teaspoonful of lemon-juice, pour over cutlets and serve. It's good for dinner.

BREAST OF VEAL STUFFED.

Obtain a breast of veal, boned and opened. For stuffing, prepare a good bread stuffing and fill your breast loosely, then sew up the opened end, braise in pan with vegetables, as for roasting, only keep your pan covered. Cook well done. Make sauce in roasting pan as for roast beef.

VEAL ROAST.

The loin of veal boned, rolled and roasted, makes a splendid dinner dish. Roast in pan with some sliced vegetables and to thicken gravy put a piece of bread in the pan which will cook to pieces and thicken the sauce, small pared potatoes baked with the meat in the same pan makes a good vegetable to serve with veal, both should be basted as often as possible.

VEAL LOAF.

Mrs. C. E. Elmes.

Six pounds of veal, chopped fine, one half pound salt pork, chopped fine, six soda crackers rolled, three eggs well beaten, pepper, salt, and sage, to taste. Mix thoroughly and roll in flour. Bake three hours, basting frequently with melted butter.

VEAL LOAF.

Mary S. Shelton.

Three pounds of raw veal, chopped fine, one half pound of salt pork chopped, three eggs, tablespoon melted butter, four Boston crackers, rolled fine, teaspoon black pepper, tablespoon salt, two teaspoons of the extract of celery, a little sage. Pack hard in a deep pan, sprinkle the top with rolled cracker, lay on bits of butter, baste while baking with water and a little butter together. Cover with a pan and bake two hours, uncover and bake till nicely browned.

VEAL POT PIE.

Cut in pieces two pounds of veal and boil in water until tender, season and add six potatoes sliced, boil until done and pour in a deep pan. Stir in a spoonful of flour, and cover with a crust made like biscuit. Bake a light brown, but be sure to have plenty of gravy in the pie.

POT PIE.

Boil two or three pounds of nice, fat beef. When nearly done add some potatoes, turnips and a head of cabbage. Cut in eight or ten pieces. Season with pepper and salt, while cooking. Serve very hot with apple sauce.

TO COOK VENISON.

Boil till tender, with sufficient water to keep from burning, when done put in some butter, pepper and salt; let it brown in the kettle, it retains all the flavor of the meat. That is the best way to cook roasts of beef; you then have juicy, tender meat.

BROWN GRAVY.

Put into a stewpan four ounces of butter rolled in flour, and an onion sliced, let them brown a few minutes, then add half a teaspoonful of grated lemon-peel, two bruised cloves, a teaspoonful of salt, half as much pepper. Add to it by degrees half a pint of water.

POULTRY.

SCIENCE OF CARVING.

An expert carver can divide poultry without removing the fork from the breast-bone or turning the bird on the dish, but a beginner will do well to have a small fork at hand for the purpose of laying cut portions aside as the carving progresses. Turn the bird so that the carving fork can be held in the left hand and firmly fixed in the breast-bone, and use a very sharp knife with a small, flexible blade. First cut off both drumsticks at the knee joint, and then remove the second joints. With a tender bird this is not a difficult matter; but both strength and skill are needed to cope successfully with a tough or under-done turkey, because very strong sinews are plentiful about the leg joints. Next cut off the first joints of the wings and the pinions, and then the joints nearest the body. This method of cutting off the first joints of the legs and wings before separating them from the body saves that troublesome feat of holding these members while they are being disjointed. Frequently they slip about the platter and spatter the dish gravy.

After the wings are removed cut off the merry-thought, or wishbone, and then the wing side bone which holds the breast to the backbone, then carve the breast in medium thin slices and serve the bird, giving gravy and stuffing on each plate. If the diners are numerous it may be necessary to cut off more of the flesh, and even to dismember the carcass, this can be done with more or less ease as the carver understands the anatomy of the bird. If a carver would study the location of the joints while carving and take the trouble to cut up several carcasses by striking the points where bones are joined together, subsequent carving would be easy. The joints of all birds are similarly placed, so nearly identical in point of junction that one is a guide to all others.

CHICKEN PIE.

Make the crust like baking-powder biscuit, only a trifle shorter. Roll half an inch thick and line a deep pudding dish with it. Have ready two small chickens, boiled till tender. Place the pieces of chicken smoothly in the pan; sprinkle salt and pepper, and a little flour over them; add a few pieces of butter, size of a hazelnut, about a large tablespoonful in all ; pour on a little of the liquor they were boiled in, then roll the top crust rather more than half inch thick; cut large stars or air holes in it. Bake till crust is thoroughly done.

PRESSED CHICKEN.

Boil one chicken until tender; chop fine; season well with pepper, salt and butter; put into a cloth; put a weight upon it and press like head cheese.

NO. 2.

Boil fowls until tender. Remove the meat from the bones and chop very fine, keeping the dark and white meat separate. Boil the liquor down until it will jelly; place in a deep buttered dish a layer of the dark meat; season with salt and pepper and cover with liquor; then a layer of white meat seasoned and cover with the liquor. Use the liquor. When full put a weight on it and it will mould firmly.

NO. 3.

Boil chickens in very little water until tender, putting plenty of salt and pepper in the water. When done separate the meat from the bones, and put it into a dish. Put the bones back into the broth and boil it down, adding, if you like, a very litte ground cloves and cinnamon. Thicken if necessary, then pour it over the chicken and press. Do not keep too much of the liquor on, and have it as thick as possible that it may jelly when cold. When it is all thoroughly cold, slice.

CHICKEN RAGOUT.

Cut a chicken into four pieces. Put in a kettle, with one-half a lemon sliced, a laurel leaf and a little thyme, pepper, salt, a tablespoon of butter and a good cup of water. Cover slowly and cook until tender. Stir one tablespoon each of flour and butter together, add a little cold water, and stir until smooth. Strain the water the chicken was cooked in, and thicken with the flour and water. When smooth and thick enough put in the chicken again and cover tightly until served.

CREAM CHICKEN WITH MUSHROOMS.

Miss M. Baldwin, Cleveland, Ohio.

One whole chicken boiled and meat cut in large squares. One-half can of mushrooms, boiled until tender. Put one-half pint of cream in sauce pan with a pinch of red pepper and one teaspoon of corn starch; then add chicken and then mushrooms after draining off the juice. Season with salt and pepper and a little butter.

FRIED CHICKEN WITH OYSTERS.

Take a nice tender chicken, open it down the back, and after cleaning it well pound all the bones flat; wash, and wipe it dry on a clean towel; then season with pepper and salt, and fry slowly in sweet lard until tender and a fine brown on both sides. Then put it on a dish where it will keep warm. Pour off the lard in the pan and any brown particles that may remain; then add one-half pint of hot water and flour enough to make the gravy of the proper consistency. Have ready about twenty-five large oysters, which remove from their liquor and put into the pan with the gravy; let them simmer until their gills begin to shrivel, observing to stir them all of the time. When done, pour them over the chicken and send to the table hot.

CHICKEN TERRAPIN.

To one boiled chicken, take nearly a pint of new milk, butter the size of an egg. Rub with the butter a tablespoon of flour until smooth. Let milk come to a boil, then add butter. Have the chicken chopped fine, add two hard boiled eggs, and pour over this the hot milk. Mix all together and heat thoroughly and add a good wine-glass of wine. Salt and pepper to taste.

DUCK DRESSING.

Stale bread, cut off all the crust; rub very fine; pour over it enough melted butter to make it crumble; salt and pepper, two small onions finely chopped.

MOCK DUCK.

Take a round of steak and spread with above dressing; roll and tie it; roast from one-half to three-quarters of an hour.

ROAST WILD DUCK.

Parboil ten minutes, putting a carrot or onion in each; remove carrot or onion; lay in fresh water one-half hour; stuff with usual dressing; roast till brown and tender, basting with butter-water and drippings; to the gravy add tablespoon currant jelly and thicken with browned flour.

BOILED GOOSE.

Dress and singe, put into a deep dish, cover with boiling milk and leave over night. In the morning wash off the milk, and put the goose into cold water on the fire; when boiling hot take it off, wash it in warm water and dry with a cloth. This process takes out the oil. Fill the body with a dressing of bread crumbs seasoned with pepper, salt, butter and two chopped onions if relished, and a little sage. Put the goose into cold water and boil gently until tender. Serve with giblet sauce, and with pickles, or acid jellies.

BONED TURKEY.

First, make the stuffing to suit the family taste. I take tenderloin, not too lean, chopped fine; a teacup of cracker crumbs,

THE MORNING NEWS.

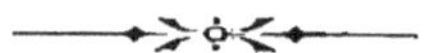

THE MORNING NEWS is the only two-cent paper in Chicago that has the service of the Associated Press. In addition to this first essential to a complete news service, its special correspondents represent it at all the principal news centers in America and Europe. It publishes "all the news," fully yet concisely. It is a 4, 6, 8, 10, 12 page paper, as occasion demands—always large enough, never too large.

THE MORNING NEWS is an independent paper. It recognizes the utility of political parties as means to the accomplishment of proper ends, but it declines to regard any mere party as a fit subject for unquestioning adoration. It is not an organ, and therefore escapes the temptation of defending or condoning the questionable under the pressure of party allegiance. It is unbiased in its presentation of all political news.

THE MORNING NEWS is a "short and to the point" paper. It believes that newspaper reading is but an incident of life, not its chief business. It accordingly leaves to the "blanket-sheets" the monopoly of tiresome and worthless amplification. It seeks to say all that the reader should care to read, and to say it in the shortest possible manner. It is a daily paper for busy people.

THE MORNING NEWS is a family newspaper. In all its departments it aims to meet the reasonable demands of every member of the family. Its reports of social life, its fashion news and much relating to the affairs of the household will especially commend it to the liking of Chicago families.

Delivered by carrier at twelve cents per week.

Send orders to

THE DAILY NEWS,

Office, 123 Fifth Avenue.

two eggs, a pint of oysters, some summer savory, pepper and salt; mix all well; have my large needle and stout thread handy, with some two-inch-wide, soft bleached old cotton cloth. Now for your turkey. It being well cleaned and singed, be careful not to break the outside skin. Cut off the legs so as to cut all the tendons where they join the drumstick. Cut the first joint from the wing; leave a good length of skin for the neck. Every bone must be taken out from the inside. Beginning with the legs, cut each ligament at the side bone joint, strip the knife close along the bone, so as to cut the flesh clean off, and draw the bone out; when both legs are boneless follow along the back, breast and wings. The neck is more difficult, but get it out nicely as you can. Now your turkey is one shapeless *slump;* but begin stuffing at the neck, from the inside; having tied securely the skin to prevent escape, fill out the wings, breast, body and legs. Now sew up the skin; bandage it in a shapely manner with your strips, not *too tight* for fear of the stuffing swelling so as to burst the skin; salt and pepper the outside and steam until perfectly tender. If it's an old chap, steam four or five hours. When done, put a tin plate and a couple of flat-irons on top of it to press until cold. Then cut in nice thin slices.

TURKEY STUFFED, GIBLET SAUCE.

Boil the gizzard of the turkey well done, put the liver and heart in hot water, for a few minutes, then fry brown in a little butter, when this is done chop all finely and put on plate ready for use. Make a sauce in pan, in which turkey is roasting, strain, skim off all fat, mix with the chopped giblets, season to taste, add a little chopped parsley, when it is ready to serve.

RICE DRESSING FOR TURKEY.

Boil rice until soft. Chop giblets fine and fry in hot butter, then add boiled rice and stir all together and put into turkey with any seasoning liked.

TURKEY GRAVY.

Heart, liver, gizzard and neck slashed and dredged thickly with flour. Put in a sauce pan with a little salt, a few peppercorns and allspice and a little mace, outside skin of three onions, lump of butter the size of a walnut. When well browned, add boiling water till of proper thinness; let it cook slowly on the back part of the stove all the morning. After removing the turkey from the dripping-pan and pouring off any grease, put the prepared gravy into the dripping-pan, and proceed to make gravy same as any.

DRESSING FOR POULTRY.

Rub fine the soft part of a loaf of bread, add one-half a pound of butter, the yolks of four eggs, one teacup full of thyme or sweet marjoram; one tablespoonful black pepper; same of salt.

JELLY SAUCE FOR GAME.

Put in a sauce pan a glass of Madeira and one-half cupful of jelly, let it dissolve, add one pint of dark sauce, as per recipe given for truffle sauce, let it come to a boil and serve.

ENTREES, ETC.

"Without good company all dainties lose their true relish, and, like painted grapes, are only seen, not tasted."

—Massinger.

DRESSING FOR CROQUETTES.

Mrs. Ewing.

One-half pint of cream or broth, one dessert spoon heaping full of flour, and one of butter. Cook until thick as batter and add the yolks of two beaten eggs, salt and pepper. One pint of chopped chicken or veal; form into croquettes, dip into bread crumbs, then into the yolk of eggs beaten with a very little water, then again into bread crumbs, and fry. It is better to use a flat camel hair brush to brush the croquettes with eggs.

CHICKEN CROQUETTES.

One plump chicken and two pounds of veal cut from the round. Boil chicken and veal separately, in cold water, just enough to cover. Pick to pieces and chop. Cut up one-third of a loaf of stale bread and soak in the broth of the chicken while warm. Put all together, and season with salt, pepper, mace and nutmeg. Beat three eggs light and mix with above ingredients. Make in oblong balls, roll them in egg and cracker crumbs, aud fry brown in equal parts of butter and lard.

NO. 2.

One solid pint of finely-chopped chicken, one table-spoonful of salt, half teaspoonful of pepper, one cupful of cream or chicken stock, one tablespoonful of flour, four eggs, one table spoonful of lemon juice, one pint of crumbs, three tablespoonsful of butter. Put cream or stock on to boil. Mix flour and butter together, and stir into the boiling cream, then add chicken and seasoning. Boil for two minutes and add two of the eggs well beaten. Take from the fire and set away to cool. When cold, shape and fry. Many people like chopped parsely or a little nutmeg.

EGG CROQUETTES.

Mrs. H. H. Brown.

Boil hard, remove the shells, roll in cracker crumbs and fry in butter until brown; make a gravy of butter, crumbs and cream and pour on them while hot. Eggs prepared in this way are a handsome dish for lunch or dinner.

POTATO CROQUETTES.

Eight potatoes mashed and beat up light, one tablespoon of butter, two eggs, and just enough milk to moisten the potatoes. Season highly with salt and pepper; flour board slightly; form potatoes in oblong shapes; roll in flour, egg and bread crumbs. Fry in lard until brown.

RICE AND MEAT CROQUETTES.

Mrs. H. H. Brown.

One cupful of boiled rice, one cupful of finely-chopped cooked meat—any kind; one teaspoonful of salt, a little pepper, two tablespoonsful of butter, half a cupful of milk, one egg. Put milk on to boil and add the meat, rice and seasoning; when this boils, add the egg, well beaten; stir one minute. After cooling, shape, dip in egg and crumbs and fry in boiling fat.

VEAL OR CHICKEN CROQUETTES—VERY EXCELLENT.

One good-sized chicken or two slices of lean veal; half a pint of cream or milk; two eggs; tablespoonful of butter; small cup of flour. After cooking meat, chop fine and season with pepper and salt; stir in first the flour, then eggs and butter; last, the milk. When well mixed, set on back part of fire and cook slowly half an hour, or until well stiffened. When cool, shape and roll in cracker crumbs, and fry. A small piece of onion size of walnut, and a piece of ham are an improvement. Should be mixed soft and cooked quickly.

VEAL CROQUETTES.

Mrs. Adams.

Chop veal very fine, add a little chopped onion and some parsley, only a very little of each. Mix one-half a cup of milk with two teaspoons of flour and a piece of butter the size of a walnut. Cook this until it thickens, then stir into the meat. Roll into balls, dip in egg and then in bread crumbs and fry like doughnuts.

LOBSTER CROQUETTES.

Chop fine one can of lobster. Put two ounces of butter in a pan to melt, stir in two ounces of flour and one-half pint of cold water till it boils. Take from fire, add cayenne pepper, salt and juice of half a lemon; stir it well. When cool take a spoonful and roll it into shape. First roll it in flour, then in egg, then in bread crumbs. Fry in hot lard.

CHICKEN CREAM.

To the broth of one chicken add one pint of cream, and the chopped breast of chicken. Thicken with one large spoonful of butter and two of flour. Add salt and pepper to taste.

BOILING EGGS.

Put the eggs in some vessel which can be closely covered, and when the teakettle boils pour in water enough to cover them; close the vessel and place it on the back part of the stove, and let it remain ten minutes. If you wish to be very exact, use a thermometer and keep the water ten minutes at exactly the heat which is indicated after the water is poured in. By the ordinary method of letting the eggs boil from two to three minutes the white part is hardened and the yolk left uncooked, or if the yolk is cooked the white is too hard. By this method the heat penetrates so gradually that the yolk is nicely cooked, while the white is soft and tender and only just done enough to be opaque.

CREAMED EGGS.

Boil three or four eggs quite hard, cut them in halves or slices. Pour over them drawn butter, as follows: One large tablespoon of butter, one large tablespoon of flour, one cup of boiling water; salt and pepper to taste.

EGG BALLS.

Boil four eggs for ten minutes, and put them into cold water When quite cold, pound them in a mortar with the beat yolk of one new egg, a teaspoonful of flour, one of chopped parsley, half a teaspoonful of salt, a quarter of a teaspoonful of cayenne, till perfectly smooth. Then form into small balls, boil them for two minutes, and add to the soup.

EGG OMELET.

Mrs. C. E. Elmes.

Eight eggs, one-half cup of milk, one tablespoon of corn starch, one-half teaspoon of salt. Beat the yolks of the eggs, add the milk and corn starch, which has been mixed with a little of the milk, salt, and last, the well-beaten white of eggs. Pour in pans well buttered and bake until brown. This quantity will make two omelets.

OMELET.

Mrs. Hammond.

Eight eggs, beaten separately, six tablespoons of milk, a little salt. Fry in butter, a piece the size of an English walnut.

NO. 2.

Beat well whites of three and yolks of six eggs separately. Mix together, a teacup new milk, or cream, one tablespoonful flour; salt and pepper to taste. Pour this on yolks and whites which have been beaten together. Melt a piece of butter in a pan. When it is hot, pour in the mixture and set the pan in a

John · J. · Leidigh · & · Co

FANCY GROCERS,

528 West Van Buren Street.

Choice Assortment of Table Luxuries
Always on Hand.

SPECIALTIES

SOLD BY THE TRADE EVERYWHERE.

COLOGNE BOUQUET	**TOILET SOAP.**	**Rare, Delicate, and Exquisitely Perfumed.**
IMPERIAL TRANSPARENT	**TOILET SOAP.**	**Very Finest Quality, Prepared Expressly for the Most Fastidious.**
VIOLET COLOGNE		**The Favorite. Pronounced by Connoisseurs to be the Perfection of Colognes.**

SOAP MAKERS—PERFUMERS—CHEMISTS,

CHICAGO.

hot oven. When it thickens, pour in the whites of the other three eggs and return to the oven, and let it brown. Slip it on a dish so that the top remains.

POACHED EGGS.

Place a frying-pan of salted boiling water on the fire, filled with as many small muffin-rings as it will hold; break the eggs singly in a cup and pour into the rings; boil them 2½ or 3 minutes; remove the rings and take up the eggs singly in a strainer; serve on half slices of nicely browned and buttered toast; put a small piece of butter on each egg; pepper slightly, and garnish with sprigs of parseley. Serve hot.

STUFFED EGGS.

A dozen eggs, boiled hard, cut in half. Take out the yolks without breaking the whites. Mash and add a huge spoonful of butter, pepper and salt, and half cup of cream. Mix well, and after setting the whites in a baking plate, fill each half with the mixture, putting the surplus in the plate, slightly brown.

CHEESE SANDWICHES.

Mrs. C. E. Crandall.

To one small bowlful of grated cheese add one large tablespoon of sweet cream, one tablespoon of melted butter and two tablespoons of Mayonnaise dressing or one teaspoon of made mustard, a little salt. Rub to a smooth cream and spread on thin slices of lightly-buttered bread or zephyr crackers if preferred.

CHEESE STRAWS, NO. 1.

First make a nice crust and roll out to a thickness of half an inch. Sprinkle thickly with grated cheese, roll up and repeat the operation, then roll out to one-third of an inch thick. Cut out some small rounds and stamp inner rounds making rings of crust, then cut the remainder into strips about five inches long and a quarter of an inch wide. Bake rings and straws on buttered tins, and in dishing them up put three or four straws inside each ring. They should be eaten hot, but may be heated over like mince pies.

CHEESE STRAWS, NO. 2.

Mary S. Shelton.

Three tablespoons of grated cheese, three tablespoons of sifted flour, three tablespoons of melted butter, one-half teaspoon of salt, one-quarter saltspoon of cayenne pepper, one-quarter saltspoon of white pepper, one yolk of egg, beaten, one tablespoon of milk. Mix the dry ingredients, then butter, milk and eggs. Roll very thin. Cut in narrow strips four inches long. Bake in slow oven fifteen minutes. Arrange in log-cabin fashion on the plate.

SALTED ALMONDS.

Blanch the nuts, but do not keep them in water any longer than necessary. To each cupful of nuts allow a teaspoonful of melted butter or salad oil. Stir well and let them stand for an hour; then sprinkle with one tablespoon of salt to a cup of nuts. Bake in moderate oven, occasionally stirring, until a delicate brown, from fifteen minutes to half an hour. Crisp when done.

MACCARONI.

Time, to boil the maccaroni, half an hour; to brown it, six or seven minutes.

Half a pound of pipe maccaroni; seven ounces of Cheshire cheese; four ounces of butter; one pint of new milk; one quart of water, and some bread-crumbs; a pinch of salt.

Flavor the milk and water with a pinch of salt, set it over the fire, and when boiling, drop in the maccaroni. When tender, drain it from the milk and water, put it into a deep dish, sprinkle the grated cheese among it with the butter.

MACCARONI WITH CHEESE, A PLAIN RECEIPT.

Boil as in the first receipt, and when drained, put into a saucepan with three tablespoonsful of grated cheese and an ounce of butter, for five minutes till well mixed; then turn it out into a dish, frost it over with grated cheese, and slightly brown the cheese in an oven, without browning the maccaroni, or it would be tough, or oiling the cheese.

WELSH RAREBIT.

Time, ten minutes. Half a pound of cheese; three tablespoonsful of ale; a thin slice of toast.

Grate the cheese fine, put to it the ale, and work it in a small saucepan over a slow fire till it is melted. Spread it on toast, and send it up boiling hot.

VEGETABLES.

Nearly all vegetables require to be cooked in boiling water. Green peas, asparagus, string beans, and those things that should retain their fresh color, should be kept uncovered while cooking. Put cabbage, cauliflower and spinach in cold water, with a little salt, for an hour before cooking. This takes out all worms or vermin.

ASPARAGUS.

Scrape. Put in water and salt, and at first boil; drop in the asparagus; boil till tender. Sauce: one yolk of egg mixed with a teaspoonful of water; a piece of butter added, and when hot, stir in two tablespoonsful of milk; pour over the drained asparagus.

BOSTON BAKED BEANS.

Mrs. Burgess.

Soak the beans over night. Put in a covered stone jar, add one-half pound salt pork streaked with lean, two tablespoons of molasses. Cover with water and cook in a slow oven a day and a night. Good for breakfast Sunday morning.

TO BOIL CARROTS.

Carrots which are stored for use are rarely out of the market, and are useful for their own quality, and much valued for ornamenting many dishes. They must be well washed for boiling, and brushed, but not peeled or scraped. If very large, cut in two parts, put them into boiling water a little salted. Boil gently till tender, usually from half an hour to an hour and a half. When boiled, rub off the skin, and slice or send them in, cut in lengths, with good melted butter.

CAULIFLOWER.

This universally-liked summer vegetable may be had from June to October, when its successor, brocoli, follows to supply the winter season. Cauliflower should be cut in the early morning while the dew hangs upon it; if this be suffered to evaporate the vegetable becomes tough and vapid. Trim the outer leaves, cut the stem away close, and plunge the vegetable into cold water salted, for an hour before it is dressed. Put a large tablespoonful of salt into boiling water and skim till the water be quite clear, or the color and appearance of the vegetable will be injured; then put the cauliflowers in, and boil slowly till they are tender, that is from fifteen to twenty-five minutes, according to size: but not one minute longer than necessary, or they will be spoiled. Drain, and serve them immediately with melted butter.

CORN PUDDING.

Split twelve ears of corn down the center of the grains, and with the back of knife scoop out the pulp. Put in a baking dish with enough cream to make the consistency of pudding, a spoonful of butter and salt to taste. Bake slowly.

GREEN CORN PUDDING.

Mrs. C. E. Crandall.

Six good sized ears green corn grated, one cup milk, three eggs, butter size of egg, salt and pepper, teaspoonful of corn starch. Bake half an hour; serve hot.

EGG PLANT.

To cook egg-plant, slice the plant one-quarter inch thick; sprinkle with salt; place layer upon layer, and let stand fifteen minutes; dip in a batter and fry in butter and lard. Another good way is to dip in egg and roll in crushed cracker and fry same way.

EGG PLANT FRIED.

Peel and slice an egg plant, roll in flour, dip in beaten eggs, (seasoned with salt and pepper) roll afterwards in cracker crumbs and fry brown in hot butter. Serve at once.

"BATAVIA"

BRAND OF

CANNED FRUITS AND VEGETABLES

Packed Fresh from the Gardens at

Batavia, in Western New York,

— THE —

Section Famous for Finest Flavor,

— AND —

Perfection in Quality Generally.

ASK YOUR GROCER FOR

"BATAVIA"

BRAND AND TAKE NO OTHER.

PRESERVED

Strawberries,
Raspberries,
Peaches,
Pears,
Quince,
Pine Apple,
Etc., Etc.

FANCY

Corn,
Tomatoes,
Peas,
Beans,
Asparagus,
Etc., Etc.

ONIONS A LA CREME.

Peel and boil some middle-sized onions in salt and water till quite tender, drain them, and throw them into a stewpan with two ounces of butter, rolled in flour; shake them round till the butter is quite dissolved, add a teaspoonful each of salt and white pepper, and then stir in by degrees as much cream as will nearly cover them. Shake the pan round, till it is on the point of boiling, then serve.

ONIONS A L'ITALIENNE.

Peel and parboil six middle-sized onions, then drain and leave them to cool. Make a small opening at the top, and scoop out a part of the inside, supplying the place with a mixture of two ounces of grated cheese, the yolks of two hard-boiled eggs chopped small, and as much grated breadcrumbs steeped in boiling cream as will suffice to fill the onions. Season with salt and pepper, and when well mixed fill the onions; dip them in beaten yolk of egg and fine breadcrumbs, and fry them a light brown. Serve them with tomato sauce.

POTATOES.

To boil old potatoes, peel thinly with a sharp knife, cut out all spots, and let them lie in cold water some hours before using. It is more economical to boil before peeling as the best part of the potato lies next to the skin. Put on in boiling water. A teaspoon of salt to every quart of water. Medium-sized potatoes will boil in half an hour. When done pour off every drop of water, cover with a clean towel and set on the back of the stove to dry for a few minutes. New potatoes require no peeling, but should merely be well washed and rubbed.

POTATOES A LA CREME.

Put into a saucepan two ounces butter, a desert spoonful of flour, some parsley and scallions (both chopped small), salt and pepper. Stir them together; add a wineglass of cream, and set on the stove, stirring constantly until it boils. Cut some boiled potatoes into slices and put into the pan with the mixture and boil all together and serve very hot.

POTATOES IN CREAM.

Boil potatoes and let them become cold, cut with a knife about the size of a pea, make a cream sauce, put the two together and season with salt, put on the stove till the whole is hot, then serve.

FANCY MASHED POTATOES.

Peel two quarts of potatoes, and when they are cooked, turn off every drop of water, put in a little salt, pepper and butter; then take a carving-fork and break them up a little; next add a little more butter, say, in the whole, a piece as large as an egg, and nearly a cup of nice milk or cream. Now take a silver fork, or three-pronged one, and beat them briskly for five minutes, or until light and creamy. They must be carried immediately to the table, or they will become heavy and clammy. If once tried this way you will never again resort to the old "masher." Remember they must be served immediately.

FRENCH FRIED POTATOES.

Pare small uncooked potatoes. Divide them in halves, and each half in three pieces. Put in the frying basket and cook in boiling fat for ten minutes. Drain, and dredge with salt. Serve hot with chops or beefsteak. Two dozen pieces can be fried at one time.

POTATO PUFFS.

Prepare the potatoes as for mashed potato. While *hot*, shape in balls about the size of an egg. Have a tin sheet well buttered, and place the balls on it. As soon as all are done, brush over with beaten egg. Brown in the oven. When done, slip a knife under them and slide them upon a hot platter. Garnish with parsley, and serve immediately.

POTATO RIBBONS.

Time, ten minutes. Wash and remove any specks from some nice large potatoes, and when peeled, lay them in cold water for a short time; then pare them round like an apple;

but do not cut the curls too thin, or they are likely to break. Fry them very slowly in butter a light color, and drain them from grease. Pile the ribbons up on a hot dish and serve.

TEXAS BAKED POTATOES.

Mrs. C. S. McHenry.

After baking medium-sized potatoes, cut lengthwise. Scrape the potatoes into a dish, being careful to reserve the half skins. Mash the potatoes. Season with pepper, salt, butter and an onion grated fine. Add a little cream or milk, and beat well. Fill the skins you have reserved, put in the oven and brown nicely.

SUCCOTASH.

Take one quart Lima beans, one-half pound pork, one and one-half dozen ears sweet corn (green); boil the pork one and one-half hours in three quarts of water, putting in the beans when the pork has boiled one-half an hour. Cut the corn off, putting it in one dish; into another scrape the milk from the cobs. When the beans are nearly done, put in the corn, and boil fifteen minutes; then add the milk from the cobs, boiling all ten minutes longer. It should be a little thicker than gruel. Stir all the time after adding the milk, or it will burn. If not sweet enough, add sugar.

TOMATOES BAKED.

Take large, smooth tomatoes, and wash all grit or sand off of them; then put them in a pan whole and place them inside of stove; let them remain in the stove just long enough to get hot through and until the skin on them cracks; then take them out, peel and cut in halves; then place in a dish and put a layer of tomatoes and sprinkle salt and pepper enough to season over them, and a teaspoonful of butter; continue in layers as above until the dish is full. Carry to the table and serve while hot.

FRIED TOMATOES.

Select the largest specimens; peel and cut in halves; have a batter made of flour, eggs and sweet milk (if you haven't the milk, water will answer as well); dip the tomatoes in this batter and fry in lard or butter; have the lard or butter hot before putting in the tomatoes. Carry to the table and serve hot.

RAW TOMATOES WITH SUGAR.

Take nice, large. smooth tomatoes; peel and cut in three slices; sprinkle sugar over them and serve before the sugar dissolves.

BROILED TOMATOES.

Cut the tomatoes in halves. Sprinkle the inside of the slices with *fine* bread crumbs; salt and pepper. Place them in the double broiler, and broil over the fire for ten minutes, having the outside next the fire. Carefully slip them on a hot dish (stone china), and put bits of butter here and there on each slice. Put the dish in the oven for ten minutes, and then serve, or, if you have a range or gas stove, brown before the fire or under the gas.

STUFFED TOMATOES.

Twelve large, smooth tomatoes, one teaspoon of salt, a little pepper, one tablespoon of butter, one of sugar, one cup of bread crumbs, one teaspoon onion juice. Arrange the tomatoes in a baking pan. Cut a thin slice from the smooth end of each. With a small spoon, scoop out as much of the pulp and juice as possible without injuring the shape. When all have been treated in this way, mix the pulp and juice with the other ingredients, and fill the tomatoes with this mixture. Put on the tops, and bake slowly three-quarters of an hour. Slide the cake turner under the tomatoes, and lift gently onto a flat dish. Garnish with parsley, and serve.

TURNIPS IN GRAVY.

Slice the turnips and put them, with two ounces of butter, into a stewpan, shaking it round till they are browned. Season with salt, pepper, a teaspoon of sugar, and a little mace. Pour over them a quarter of a pint of good brown gravy, and when quite hot serve them in it.

GREEN VEGETABLES.

Boil green vegetables in salted water until done, and then put in cold water. You can keep green vegetables fresh this way for several days. Use them afterward in a like manner as canned vegeabtles.

St. Benedictus Olive Oil

Is a Sublime Virgin Oil of excellent flavor, pressed from selected olives. Palatable and nutricious, grateful to the system, beneficial in many diseases. It is specially recommended by the medical profession. For salads and for table purposes generally it stands pre-eminent. **C. JEVNE & CO., Agents,** Importers and Grocers, 110 and 112 Madison Street, Chicago; and 95 East Third Street, St. Paul.

FRANCIS SQUAIR,

Manufacturing and Dispensing Chemist,

DEALER IN

Fine Toilet Requisites, Proprietary Articles, Perfumery, Etc.

MANUFACTURER OF

Squair's "Perfection" Kumyss,

30 cents a bottle, $3.25 per dozen.

567 W. Madison St., N. E. Cor. Ogden Ave.

SALADS.

CREAM DRESSING FOR SALADS.

Mrs. J. R. Lyons.

One cup sweet cream, it must be perfectly fresh; one tablespoonful corn starch, or very fine flour; whites of two eggs, beaten stiff; three tablespoonfuls vinegar, two tablespoonfuls best salad oil (four tablespoonfuls melted butter is better), two teaspoonfuls powdered sugar, one teaspoonful (scant) of salt, half a teaspoonful pepper, one teaspoonful made mustard. Heat cream almost to boiling; stir in the flour, previously wet with cold milk; boil two minutes, stirring all the time; add the sugar, and take from fire. When half cold beat in whipped whites of eggs. Set aside to cool. When quite cold, whip in the oil, pepper, mustard and salt, and if salad is ready add the vinegar, and pour at once over it; especially nice for lettuce. If for chickens, use only white meat.

CREAM SALAD DRESSING.

Mr. De L. B.

Half a cupful of vinegar, two teaspoonsful of mustard, three eggs, one cupful of cream. Scald the vinegar and mustard, and let it cool a little, then add the eggs beaten very light, lastly add the cream. Cook in a farina kettle until it is the consistency of boiled custard.

SALAD DRESSING.

Mrs. D. R. B.

Yolks of four eggs, five tablespoons of Lucca oil (sweet oil), one cup of new cold milk, one half cup of vinegar, salt, mustard and pepper. Beat the eggs and oil *slowly* together, add milk and vinegar. Set the saucepan on the fire until the mixture becomes thick, stirring all the time. Set away to cool. When cold, season with the salt, mustard and pepper.

SALAD DRESSING.

Yolks of four eggs, two-thirds cup vinegar, one teaspoonful salt, one and a half teaspoonfuls made mustard. Mix the vinegar, mustard and salt well together and add the yolks, well beaten, just before putting on the fire. Boil and stir rapidly. When done it should be smooth and thick. When cool add four tablespoonsful salad oil, and one half cup of cream.

CELERY SAUCE.

Cut the tender parts of a head of celery very fine. Pour on water enough to cover them and no more. Cover the saucepan and set where it will simmer an hour. Mix together two tablespoonsful of flour and four of butter, When the celery has been boiling one hour, add to it the butter and flour, one pint of milk or cream, and salt and pepper.. Boil up once, and serve.

HOLLANDAISE SAUCE.

Half a teacupful of butter, the juice of half a lemon, the yolks of two eggs, a speck of cayenne, half a cupful of boiling water, half a teaspoonful of salt. Beat the butter to a cream; then add the yolks, one by one, the lemon-juice, pepper and salt. Place the bowl in which these are mixed in a saucepan of boiling water. Beat with an egg-beater until the sauce begins to thicken (about a minute), and add the boiling water, beating all the time. When like soft custard it is done. This sauce is nice for meat or fish.

MAYONAISE SAUCE.

Take the yolks of three raw eggs, one even tablespoon of mustard, one of sugar, one teaspoon of salt, and pepper to taste. Break the yolks into a bowl; beat a few strokes, and add gradually the mustard, sugar, salt and pepper. Take one-half of a pint bottle of the best olive oil and stir in a few drops at a time. The sauce will become firm like jelly. When one-half of the half pint is used add the juice of one lemon by degrees with the

remainder of the oil, then add a quarter of a cup of good vinegar. This is good with chicken, salmon or vegetable salad, and will keep for weeks.

MUSTARD SAUCE.

Mustard is considered to be one of the most wholesome of condiments. It is always best to prepare it in small quantities, and send it up quite fresh. It should be smoothly blended with milk or cream, to which a small portion of salt may be added, till reduced to the proper consistency. If required piquant, vinegar or horseradish vinegar may be substituted for the milk.

CABBAGE DRESSING.

M. J. Hodge.

Teacup vinegar, tablespoon butter, same of flour, two teaspoons of sugar, pepper and salt to taste. Cook and place over cabbage hot, cover close, and eat cold.

TOMATO SAUCE.

One quart of canned tomatoes, two tablespoons of butter, two of flour, eight cloves and a small slice of onion. Cook tomato, onion and cloves ten minutes. Heat the butter in a small frying-pan, and add the flour. Stir over the fire until smooth and brown, and then stir into the tomatoes. Cook two minutes. Season to taste with salt and pepper, and rub through a strainer fine enough to keep back the seeds. This sauce is nice for fish, meat and maccaroni.

SAUCE OF TOMATOES.

Mrs. H. S. Clay.

One gallon tomatoes peeled; add two tablespoons mustard seed, one teaspoon cayenne pepper, one teaspoon allspice, one teaspoon cloves, one gill salt, four or five onions chopped fine, one pint brown sugar, one quart vinegar. Boil, stirring till of the consistency of marmalade. Bottle and seal.

CHICKEN CURRY.

One chicken, weighing three pounds, three-fourths of a cupful of butter, two large onions, one heaping tablespoonful of curry powder; three tomatoes, or one cupful of the canned article, enough cayenne to cover a silver three-cent piece, salt, one cupful of milk. Put the butter and the onions, cut fine, on to cook. Stir until brown; then put in the chicken, which has been cut in small pieces, the curry, tomatoes, salt and pepper. Stir well, cover tightly, and let simmer one hour, stirring occasionally, then add the milk. Boil up once and serve with boiled rice. This makes a very rich and hot curry.

CHICKEN SALAD.

The white meat of a chicken, the weight in celery, the yolk of one raw egg and one hard-boiled, a teaspoonful of salt, the same of pepper, half a teaspoonful of mustard, a tablespoonful of salad oil, one of white wine vinegar, one teaspoonful of extract of celery.

Take the white meat of a chicken, boiled, cut it small, or mince it fine; take the same quantity, or *more*, of white tender celery cut small, and mix the celery and chicken together an hour or two before it is wanted, then add the dressing made thus: Break the yolk of a hard-boiled egg very fine with a silver fork, add to it the yolk of a raw egg, and the pepper and salt, with half a tablespoonful of made mustard: work all smoothly together, adding gradually a tablespoonful of salad oil, and the same of white wine vinegar. Mix the chicken with the dressing, pile it up in the dish, and spread some of the dressing over the outside. Garnish with the delicate leaves of the celery, the white of the egg cut into rings, green pickles cut in slices, pickled beet root in slices and stars, and placed alternately with the rings of egg and the leaves.

LOBSTER SALAD.

A lobster, yolks of two eggs, a spoonful of made mustard, three tablespoons of salad oil, a taste of vinegar, a little salt, some fresh lettuces or celery.

Pick all the meat out of the lobster, thoroughly beat the yolks of two new-laid eggs, beat in made mustard to taste, and continuing to beat them, drop in three tablespoonfuls of salad oil; add whatever flavoring may be preferred, a taste of vinegar, and some salt. Mix in six tablespoonsful of vinegar, and the soft part of the lobster. Moisten the remainder of the lobster with this, and lay it at the bottom of the bowl; cut up the lettuce, take care that it is well rolled over in the dressing, and put it over the lobster. Mustard can be left out if it is not liked. The above quantity is given for the proportions, and can be increased according to the lobster employed.

SHRIMP SALAD.

Open a can of shrimps some hours before you want to use them and turn upon a dish. Set on ice until needed. Line a salad bowl or a bread salver with leaves of cool, crisp lettuce; lay the shrimps on them and pour mayonaise dressing on the fish, or send it around with the salad. A popular dish in hot weather.

POTATO SALAD.

Three or four cold boiled potatoes sliced in small squares or pieces, quarter of small onion chopped very fine; mix both together. Dressing, three eggs beaten light, one half teaspoon black pepper, one half teaspoon salt, one teaspoon made mustard, shake of red pepper, one tablespoon melted butter and two tablespoons sweet oil, a quarter cup of cream, one large half cup vinegar. Make this in farina kettle, beat well together and stir constantly until it thickens.

STUFFED OLIVES.

Remove the pit carefully and fill with sardines minced fine.

COMBINATIONS FOR SALADS.

1. Lettuce with water cresses or pepper grass mixed, and small radishes placed around for garnish. Clear dressing.

2. Lettuce with celery mixed. Cut the celery into pieces an inch and a half long, then slice these lengthwise into four or five pieces. Mix with lettuce. Mayonaise dressing.

3. Lettuce and slices of cold boiled potatoes and cold boiled beets. Potatoes piled in the center, beets next and lettuce around the outside of the dish. Potato salad dressing.

4. Celery cut into small pieces. Mayonaise dressing.

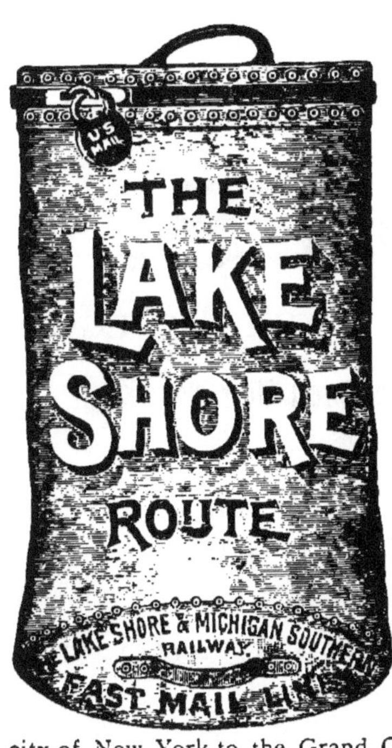

THE LAKE SHORE ROUTE

—BETWEEN—

CHICAGO

—AND—

NEW YORK, BOSTON

AND THE EAST,

COMPOSED OF THE

Lake Shore, New York Central & Boston and Albany Railroads,

Is recognized as embodying in its equipment, roadbed and service all that is essential to comfort, convenience and luxury in railway transportation. It is the only double track route to New York and Boston; carries passengers into the city of New York to the Grand Central Depot without subjecting them to the annoyance of a transfer, and is the only route possessing that advantage.

Wagner Palace Sleeping Cars are run through without change to New York and Boston.

The celebrated "Chicago and New York Limited" trains run *via* the Lake Shore Route. These trains are certainly the easiest riding and handsomest ever constructed for long distance service. They are composed of new and beautiful Sleeping, Drawing Room, Dining and Buffet Smoking Cars, constructed with that best of modern railway contrivances, the enclosed vestibule on the platforms, and heated by steam from the locomotive. The commendable feature of the vestibule is the security it lends to the hitherto hazardous undertaking of moving from car to car. By it a train is practically converted into one long car of several compartments, and one may walk from one end of the train to the other without concern as to personal safety, and without the slightest exposure to the elements.

The steam heating apparatus is admirable, the temperature in the cars being maintained at a uniform comfortable degree throughout. These facts should be remembered when a trip is to be made, and tickets purchased *via* the

LAKE SHORE ROUTE.

PICKLES.

CABBAGE PICKLE.

Mrs. G. Cunningham.

Scald the quartered heads in a strong brine, and squeeze perfectly dry in a towel, put in a jar and pour cold vinegar over, put a quantity of white mustard seed and pod pepper with it, color the brine deeply with turmeric.

PICKLED CABBAGE.

No. 2.

Select a nice, firm head of cabbage; take off all the outside leaves and shave it exceedingly fine (not chop it, remember); place it in the jar you intend to keep it in, sprinkle salt and pepper on it to your taste, then cut a couple of red peppers very fine; add two tablespoonsful celery seed (or it is a great improvement, if you can get it, to chop up fine two heads of nice celery), two tablespoons white mustard seed; pour over cold vinegar enough to cover.

CUCUMBER PICKLES.

Mrs. Boyles.

Wash the cucumbers, put in a jar and cover with water. For every one hundred pickles allow one pint of salt. Let them stand twenty-four hours. Then drain off the brine and wipe dry. Take the same quantity of vinegar there was of brine. Scald it, then pour over the pickles; let them stand twenty-four hours. Take the same vinegar and scald again, and pour over the pickles. Let them stand twenty-four hours longer. The last day dry each pickle, and lay them in the jar they are to be kept in. Take-fresh vinegar the same quantity and boil together with one half pound of sugar, ounce of whole pepper, an ounce of whole allspice, an ounce of whole cloves and a lump of alum half as big as an hen's egg (alum is to harden the pickle). Pour over the pickles and cover tight. In a few days they will be ready to eat.

CUCUMBER PICKLES.

Make a brine of *rock* salt strong enough to bear an egg. When boiling hot pour it on six hundred cucumbers. Let stand twenty-four hours: then wash in clear, cold water and dry. Scald vinegar and pour over them; let stand twenty-four hours, then throw that off, take fresh vinegar, one quart brown sugar, two green peppers, half pint mustard seed, six cents worth ginger root, one tablespoon celery seed, cinnamon, cloves, allspice each, piece of alum size of a nut powdered fine. Scald altogether, pour over boiling water.

SWEET CUCUMBER PICKLES.

Take small crock of pickled cucumbers and make a good rich syrup of New Orleans molasses, and cider vinegar, and whole cloves; heat together and turn over them, and in two days you will have a most delicious, brittle, hard, sweet pickle.

RIPE CUCUMBER PICKLES.

Remove the seeds and rinds; slice them an inch thick; soak them in cold vinegar over night; drain off the vinegar and throw it away. Take one gallon of vinegar, four pounds of sugar, a few sticks of cinnamon bark, and in this mixture boil the pieces of cucumbers, removing each piece as it becomes clear, without being broken—some pieces will be done before others, and place them in a jar; when all are removed to the jar pour the boiling vinegar over them, and keep them under the surface.

MIXED PICKLES.

Mrs. Boyles.

Two heads of cabbage sliced fine and cut into inch pieces, two heads of cauliflower torn into inch pieces, slice fifty cucumbers about three inches long, some grated and some in round pieces about one quarter inch in thickness, four quarts of string beans, boiled until tender in salted water, eight large green peppers with the seeds taken out cut up into small pieces, one quart of small white onions. Pour over all, excepting string beans, a strong brine and let stand twenty-four hours. Drain or squeeze well. For a three-gallon jar take six quarts of vinegar, one teaspoon cayenne pepper, quarter pound white pepper ground, one tablespoon turmeric powder, quarter pound whole mustard seed, a piece of alum half size of an egg. Pour vinegar and spices hot over all. When cold, add a pint of made mustard. Stir thoroughly.

OLIVE OIL PICKLES.

Mrs. J. E. Montrose.

One hundred small cucumbers sliced, three pints small onions sliced, three ounces celery seed, four ounces white mustard seed, two ounces whole white pepper, one pint olive oil, a piece of alum dissolved in the vinegar. Lay the cucumbers in soft water three hours, drain and mix with the onions, then add oil, mix thoroughly, then add seeds: mix well together and pour cold vinegar over all. The directions must be followed explicitly.

CHILI SAUCE.

Take two quarts of ripe tomatoes, four large onions and four red peppers. Chop them together; then add four cups of vinegar, three tablespoons of salt, two teaspoons each of cloves, ground cinnamon, ginger, allspice and nutmeg. Boil all together for one hour, and bottle for use after straining through a sieve or coarse netting. Is equal to famous Worcestershire.

PICCALILLI.

Mrs. George Cunningham, Nashville, Tenn.

First pickle the articles you wish to use—cucumbers, cauliflower, cottage onions and string beans, if desired. In the dressing take a gallon of the vinegar which has been on the cabbage already spiced, equal quantities, about a teacupful of the best English mustard, flour and sugar, and nearly as much turmeric. Mix in a smooth paste with some of the vinegar. Let the vinegar come to a boil, and stir this mixture in, on the fire, and cook till a smooth cream. Slice the different pickles. leaving the small onions while putting them in a crock with a good deal of celery seed (pounded) and white mustard seed. Pour the dressing over while hot and cover closely.

PICCALILLI.

Mrs. Boyles.

Slice one peck of green tomatoes: salt them in layers; let them drain over night, then take three teaspoons of ground mustard, one teaspoon of ground pepper, two teaspoons of ground cloves, two teaspoons of ground cinnamon, four peppers chopped fine. Mix with one-fourth pint whole mustard, one cup sugar, two quarts of vinegar. Put into a porcelain kettle. let come to a boil; add tomatoes: let boil one-half hour or more.

CHOW CHOW.

Two quarts of small white onions, two quarts of gherkins, two quarts of string beans, two small cauliflowers, one-half a dozen ripe red peppers, one half pound mustard séed, one-half pound of whole pepper, one pound ground mustard and, as there is nothing so adulterated as ground mustard, it's better to get it at the druggist's; twenty or thirty bay leaves, and two quarts of good cider or wine vinegar. Peel the onions, halve the cucumbers, string the beans, and cut in pieces the cauliflower. Put all in a wooden tray, and sprinkle well with salt. In the morning

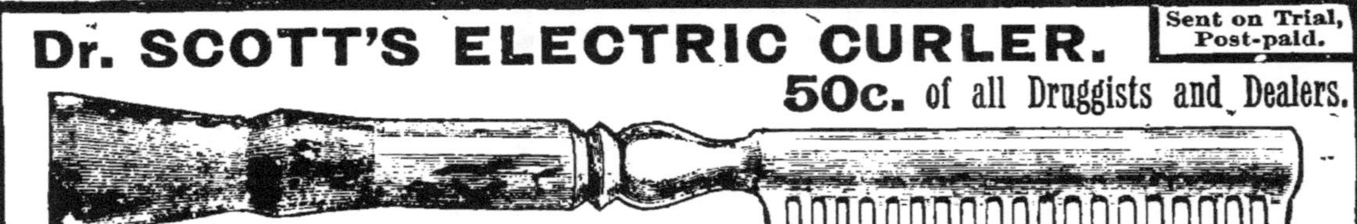

EDWARD J. HILL. RICHARD W. HILL.

E. J. Hill & Son,

ATTORNEYS AND COUNSELORS,

128 South Clark Street,

CHICAGO, ILL.

MISS SARA REIDY,

DEALER IN

Hair Goods and Hair Ornaments,

34 Monroe St., near Wabash Av.,

CHICAGO.

A Competent Hairdresser from Paris in Attendance.

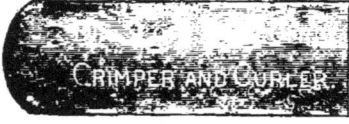

wash and drain thoroughly, and put all into the cold vinegar, except the red peppers. Let boil twenty minutes slowly, frequently turning over. Have wax melted in a deep dish, and, as you fill and cork up, dip into the wax. The peppers you can put in to show to the best advantage.

GREEN TOMATO PICKLE.

Mrs. C. Stearns.

One peck of green tomatoes, and six large onions, sliced. Sprinkle with one cupful of salt, and let stand over night. In the morning drain. Add to the tomatoes two quarts of water and one quart of vinegar. Boil fifteen minutes, then drain again and throw this vinegar and water away. Add to the pickle two pounds of sugar, two quarts of vinegar two tablespoonfuls each of clove, allspice, ginger, mustard, cinnamon. Boil fifteen minutes.

TOMATO PICKLES.

Mrs. Andrews.

Half peck green peppers. two and a half pecks green tomatoes, five large onions, chopped, two and a half cups of salt. Let stand over night and drain; in the morning add five quarts vinegar and boil fifteen minutes. Then add three and a half pounds of brown sugar, three-quarters of a pound of mustard seed, five tablespoons cinnamon, two and a half tablespoons allspice, two tablespoons cloves, three tablespoons ginger, three tablespoons celery seed. After all is prepared, boil twenty minutes.

PICKLED EGGS.

Select nine fresh ones, boil them hard, lift them directly from the hot water into cold. When cool, remove the shell, stick cloves into them, and drop in cold vinegar.

PICKLED PEACHES.

Mrs. Ryer.

Seven pounds of peaches, three and half pounds of sugar, one half pint of vinegar, one ounce of cinnamon, one ounce of cloves. Make syrup, and pour over peaches. Let stand for twenty-four hours, and boil together.

FRENCH CATSUP.

Mrs. C. E. Elmes.

One peck of tomatoes, six onions, chopped very fine, two tablespoonsful each of allspice, cloves, black pepper, two ounces of celery and one quarter of a pound of salt, one half pound of brown sugar, one quart of strong vinegar. Boil all together until thick enough.

OYSTER CATSUP.

Select eighteen or twenty large fresh oysters, drain off the liquor and pound them in a mortar; then put them in a stew-pan together with their liquor, adding a tumbler of sherry, four ounces of anchovies, the rind of half a lemon pared very thin, half a saltspoon of pounded mace and half a dozen pep-percorns. Place the pan on the fire and let the contents simmer gently for half an hour, then remove it, and when cold bottle for use.

Large green peppers are relished prepared in this way: Re-move all the seeds and fill the pepper with cooked tomato pulp and minced mushrooms, seasoning with salt and butter. Bake in a hot oven and serve.

TOMATO CATSUP.

Mrs. West.

One half bushel tomatoes, twelve onions, one teacup salt, one teacup white pepper, one teacup mustard, one quarter tea-cup red pepper, one pound brown sugar. Put tomatoes and onions sliced to boil. When soft strain and add the seasoning. When it has boiled down to one third it is done. When cool add sufficient to taste and make thin enough to pour in bottles. Very fine.

TOMATO CATSUP.

Wash the tomatoes and break them open unpared. Put them in a large tin and let them boil, then drain them through a sieve dry as possible, getting all the pulp and leaving only the skin and seeds. To every gallon put two tablespoonfuls of salt, four tablespoonfuls of pepper, two of mustard, one of all-spice, one and one half of cloves, four of cinnamon, a little sugar and a pint of vinegar. Boil two or three hours and bottle tight.

MUSTARD FOR MEAT.

The yolk of one egg, well beaten, one half teaspoonful salt, one teaspoonful butter, one tablespoonful mustard, and enough vinegar to make it the proper consistency.

BREAD, ETC.

"He is crowned with all achieving who perceives and then performs."
—Goethe.

YEAST.

One quart boiling water poured upon a cup of grated raw potatoes, with a small infusion of hops. Add one half teacup of salt, one half teacup of sugar and a little yeast to raise it. Keep it warm until it raises. Brewer's yeast is the best unless you have some of the same yeast.

YEAST.

Twelve good sized potatoes, one gallon water when done, two handfuls hops in a bag, one tablespoon ginger, two teacups sugar, one of salt. Boil potatoes and hops, strain, then add the other ingredients and scald well. Put into a jug and cork tight. One cupful makes four loaves.

YEAST.

Grate ten large potatoes raw; have ready six quarts of strong hop tea boiling; pour over the potatoes, stirring constantly, and let it boil a moment or two; add one coffee cup of salt and sugar each. When milk-warm raise with a pint of baker's or home-made yeast. Set in a warm place until done working. This is an excellent recipe, and will keep a long time in a cool place.

BREAD MADE EASY.

Mrs. H. H. Brown.

Three quarts flour, small tablespoon salt. Mix with quite hot water. Stirring quickly, dissolve the yeast in a little warm water, and stir in when sufficiently cool. Beat hard and long. Let it stand one night when warm. In the morning mold and put into pans. Let it stand awhile before putting into oven.

LIGHT BREAD.

Two quarts of scalded "Cerealine," eight tablespoonfuls of lard, six ounces of Fleischmann's yeast, eight quarts of flour, four teaspoonfuls of salt.

Mix the wheat flour and "Cerealine" together; dissolve the salt in water, and dissolve six ounces of Fleischmann's yeast in a little cold water, and make into a stiff dough. Allow this mixture to raise about three hours, and then take out and make into six loaves of bread, and set in a pan until it raises again, then bake about an hour in a hot oven.

POTATO BREAD.

Time to bake, one and a half to two hours.

Two and a half pounds of mealy potatoes, seven pounds of flour, a quarter of a pint of yeast, two ounces of salt.

Boil two pounds and a half of nice mealy potatoes till floury; rub and mash them smooth; then mix them with sufficient cold water to let them pass through a coarse sieve, and any lump that remains must be again mashed and pressed through. Mix this paste with the yeast, and then add it to the flour. Set it to rise, well knead it, and make it into a stiff, tough dough.

BREAD FOR DYSPEPTICS.

For one loaf: one pint attrition flour, one pint wheat flour; prepare with Horsford's Bread Preparation according to directions which come with it, adding salt, mixing soft, with sweet milk, with the hands, and bake quickly. To be used when a day old.

Ask Your Grocer for the

ALDRICH BAKERY

"A. B. C."

B-R-E-A-D

N. B.—None Genuine without the letters "A. B. C." on top of the loaf.

This Bread is Guaranteed the Best that can be made.

SALT YEAST BREAD.

Mrs. H. J. Jones.

One teacup sweet milk, boil and stir in two tablespoons meal while hot at night. Next morning add one cup hot water, one full cup of flour, one tablespoon sugar, one teaspoon salt to the milk; mix well. Put in a vessel in a warm place; when light, take three quarts sifted flour; large spoonful of lard, a little more salt; mix as soft as you can kneed, which do thoroughly until it thickens. Let it rise and bake in quick oven.

BROWN BREAD.

One quart oatmeal scalded, one quart ryemeal or graham flour; one cup yeast, one cup molasses, large teaspoonful salt, small teaspoonful soda. Put in pan, let it rise; bake five hours.

CORN BREAD.

Mrs. Hammond.

Two cups corn meal, one cup flour, one teaspoonful salt, one tablespoonful sugar, two eggs, two cups milk, one heaping spoonful baking powder; and half as much more, dry in flour.

CORN BREAD.

One cup of "Cerealine," one and a half pints of corn meal, one teaspoon of salt, three eggs, one and one-fourth pints of milk, one tablespoon of sugar, one-half pint of flour, two teaspoons of baking powder; two tablespoons of lard. Sift the corn meal, flour, sugar, salt, and baking powder together; rub in the lard cold; add eggs, well beaten, milk, and "Cerealine"; mix into a moderately stiff batter; pour it from the bowl into a shallow cake pan, and bake in a rather hot oven.

STEAMED BROWN BREAD.

Mrs. Hill.

Two coffee cups cornmeal, two coffee cups graham flour, two-thirds coffee cup New Orleans molasses, two eggs, small spoon salt, one teaspoon soda stirred into the molasses until it is all foam, and milk to form a soft batter. Steam three hours.

BROWN BREAD.

Mrs. Raymond, Boston.

One quart milk, two cups of ryemeal, three cups of Indian meal, one cup of molasses, one tablespoon of salt. one tablespoon of soda. Steam or bake two and a half hours.

BROWN BREAD.

Mrs. Lason.

One-half teaspoon soda dissolved in a little warm water, one cup sour milk, put soda in one-half cup molasses, little salt, one egg or two yolks and one white, graham flour (and a little wheat flour); don't put too much flour in, mix lightly. Steam one and a half hours. Keep water boiling constantly.

BREAKFAST COFFEE CAKES.

Three cups bread sponge, one-half cup butter, little sugar, one egg. Roll thin as baking powder biscuit. Cut out with tumbler or cake-cutter; sprinkle over a little sugar, cinnamon, and little bits of butter. As our family is small, I only use one-half the recipe.

ALBANY BREAKFAST CAKES.

Time, half an hour. Six eggs, one quart of milk, a teaspoonful of salt; a piece of saleratus the size of two peas, and sufficient flour to make a thick batter.

Beat the eggs very light, and stir them into a quart of milk. Add the salt and salaratus, dissolved in a little hot water. Stir in sufficient flour to make a thick batter, rub some small tins the size of a tea-saucer with butter, and half fill them with the batter. Bake them in a quick oven.

"JOHNNY CAKE."

A Recipe by Bishop Williams, of Connecticutt.

A forgetful old Bishop, all broken to pieces,
Neglected to dish up for one of his nieces
A recipe for "corn-pone," the best ever known.
So he hastes to repair his sin of omission,
And hopes that in view of his shattered condition
His suit for forgiveness, he humbly may urge,
So here's the recipe—and it comes from Lake George.

Take a cup of corn meal, and the meal should be yellow,
Add a cup of wheat flour, for to make the corn mellow;
Of sugar a cup, white or brown, at your pleasure,
(The color is nothing, the point is the measure.)

And now comes the troublesome thing to indite,
For the rhyme and the reason they trouble me quite,
For after the sugar, the flour and the meal—
Comes a cup of sour cream, but, unless you should steal—
From your neighbors I fear you will never be able—
This item to put upon your cooks' table.

For sure and indeed in all towns I remember,
Sour cream is as scarce as June bugs in December.
So here an alternative nicely contrived,
Is suggested at once your mind to relieve,
And showing how you without stealing at all,
The ground that seemed lost, may retrieve.
Instead of sour cream, take one cup of milk,
"Sweet milk," what a sweet phrase to utter.
And to make it cream like, put into the cup
Just three tablespoonsful of butter,
Cream of tartar, one teaspoonful, rule dietetic,
How nearly I wrote it down, "tartar emetic."
But no: cream of tartar it is without doubt,
And so the alternative makes itself out.

Of soda, the half of a teaspoonful add—
Or else your poor corn cake will go to the bad.
Two eggs must be broken without being beat,
Then of salt a teaspoonful, your work will complete.
Twenty minutes of baking are needful to bring
To the point of perfection this "awful good thing."

To eat at the best, this remarkable cake—
You should fish all day long on the royal named lake,
With the bright water-glancing in glorious light,
And beauties unnumbered bewildering your sight.
On mountain and lake, in water and sky,
And then when the shadow falls down from on high.
"Seek Sabbath Day Point" as light fades away—
And end with this feast the angels long day.
Then, then you will find without any question
That an appetite honest waits on digestion.

ENGLISH BREAKFAST CAKE.

One cup milk, one tablespoonful of butter, one tablespoonful sugar, one egg, one pint flour, one teaspoonful cream tartar, one-half teaspoonful soda.

BREAD GRIDDLE CAKES.

Mrs. LeRoy.

Put three slices of dried bread to soak over night in some milk. In the morning add two eggs well beaten, one teaspoon of soda, a good cup of flour and a little salt.

SOUR MILK GRIDDLE CAKES.

One quart of sour milk, one large teaspoonful soda, one teaspoonful salt, two eggs, flour enough to make a thin batter.

GRAHAM BREAD.

Mrs. Hayes.

One quart warm water, one-third teacup syrup, one teaspoonful salt, one half cup yeast. Make as thick with graham flour as can be stirred with a spoon.

GRAHAM BREAD.

One pint yeast, same as used for white bread, stir in a pint of warm water and a little salt, then add graham flour unil you have a thick batter. Bake fifteen minutes longer than the same size loaf of white bread. It will not rise as much as other bread.

GRAHAM BREAD.

Take the "sponge" of white bread when light, enough for one loaf or two, as you wish, and mix in enough graham flour to make a moderately stiff loaf; place in a pan, and, when light, bake. You can add a little sugar or molasses if you like. Can also make very nice rye bread in the same way.

GRAHAM BREAD.

Graham three quarts, two quarts warm water, one half pint yeast, one teaspoonful soda, one half pint sugar. Mix with a spoon. Pour into deep tins, well greased, and set in a warm place till quite light. Bake with a steady moderate heat two hours. This recipe makes three good loaves.

GRAHAM PUFFS.

One egg, one pint sweet milk, one pint graham flour and a pinch of salt; beat the egg thoroughly; add the milk, then the flour gradually; beat the whole mixture briskly with an egg beater; pour into cast-iron gem pans, well greased and piping hot; bake in a very hot oven. This mixture is just sufficient for twelve gems.

GRAHAM PUFFS.

Sift together one and one half pints of graham flour, one teaspoonful of salt and three teaspoonfuls of baking powder. Mix with this one pint of milk and two well-beaten eggs until a smooth batter is obtained. Fill cold, well greased gem pans half full with the batter, and bake in a hot oven for ten minutes.

GRAHAM CAKES.

Mrs. Raymond, Boston.

One cup graham, one cup flour, one egg, one cup of milk, a little salt and sugar.

GRAHAM OR RYE MUSH.

Stir graham or rye meal into boiling water, with a little salt, till quite thick; cook a few minutes. This is very nice either with poached eggs or butter and sugar.

OATMEAL MUSH.

Soak the oatmeal over night in enough water to wet it, in the morning stir into boiling water. Cook a few minutes.

CRACKED WHEAT.

Stir five large heaping spoonfuls of the crushed white wheat sold by grocers into a quart of boiling water, and set the tin pail holding it into a pan of boiling water to cook twenty minutes. This prevents it burning, and is a cheap and easy substitute for a farina kettle. Salt well, and when the kernels have swelled and burst like popcorn it is done. Serve it plain to eat with meat and gravy like rice, or add half a teaspoonful of cinnamon, a pinch of ground cloves, a handful of raisins or currants, and a half cup of sugar while boiling, and you have a savory breakfast dish. Sometimes we serve it plain in saucers, with a dust of cinnamon on the top, and sugar and utter or cream, as German pancake is eaten.

GRIDDLE CAKES.

Three cupfuls of "Cerealine," one teaspoonful salt, one egg, two cupfuls of milk, one teaspoonful baking powder.

Mix the salt and baking powder thoroughly with the "Cerealine;" add the well-beaten egg to the milk, and pour on to the Cerealine Flake; stir all together until well mixed; fry on a well greased griddle, over a good fire; fry to a nice brown on one side, and then turn and fry as before and serve hot with maple syrup.

HOMINY BALLS.

One cup of fine hominy, boil until thoroughly cooked. When cold, add one beaten egg and a small piece of butter, a little salt. Make into balls by flouring the hands. Drop into a kettle of hot lard. To be eaten with maple syrup.

HOMINY BREAD.

Mrs. H. J. Jones.

Take cold boiled hominy (grits) and add one egg, teaspoon of butter, salt to taste, and milk to make like pudding batter. Bake in a baking dish for breakfast.

BAKED HOMINY GRITS.

Miss Lovejoy.

One quart milk, one cup grits, two eggs and salt. When the milk and salt boil, stir in grits and boil one half hour. When cool beat the eggs, and beat them well into hominy. Bake one half hour.

MUFFINS.

One pint of milk, three tablespoonsful of yeast, make a thin batter. In the morning add one egg and one spoonful of sugar. Bake in cups.

MUFFINS.

Mrs. H. L. Hammond.

Three-quarters pint milk, one pint flour, one heaping teaspoonful baking powdef, one-half teaspoonful salt, two eggs, butter size of an egg.

EGGLESS MUFFINS.

Mrs. Oakley.

Half a cupful of butter, two cupsful of sweet milk, three teaspoonsful of baking powder, one scant quart of flour, a pinch of salt, a quarter of a cupful of sugar.

MUFFINS ENGLISH STYLE.

One pint of "Cerealine," a little salt, two and one half teaspoonfuls of baking powder, one and three-fourths pints of flour, one tablespoonful sugar, one and one-fourth pints of light cream. Sift the flour, salt, sugar and baking powder together; add the milk and "Cerealine," and mix into a smooth batter, a little stiffer than for griddle cakes; have the griddle heated evenly all over; grease it and lay the muffin rings on the griddle; fill them half full, and when risen well up to the top of the rings, turn them over gently with a cake turner; they should not bake brown, but of a nice buff color; when all are cooked, pull each one open in half, and toast delicately; butter well, and serve on folded napkin, piled high and very hot.

QUICK MUFFINS.

One cup milk, one cup flour, one egg, well beaten, salt. Have your gem-irons very hot; fill one-half full and bake quickly. These are delicious with good butter and maple syrup.

RAISED MUFFINS.

Two large tablespoons of sugar, one tablespoon of butter, beat together, add two eggs, well beaten, a good pinch of salt. dissolve one-half cake yeast in one pint of warm milk, stir all together, add enough flour to make a stiff batter. Make up the muffins as late as possible in the evening, let rise over night. About an hour before breakfast, put in well greased muffin rings; let rise about half an hour; bake twenty minutes in a quick oven. Fill the rings about half full.

SWISS MUFFINS.

One quart flour, two eggs, one teaspoon sugar, one tablespoon, lard, one tablespoon butter, one-half cup yeast; mix well with one cup milk. Let it rise, work and roll out about half an inch thick. Cut one larger than the other, place small one on top, with melted butter between. Let rise and bake.

OATMEAL CAKES.

One cup rather fine oat-meal; three cups water, stirred together and allowed to swell. Butter a pie-tin, and turn the batter in, and bake half an hour, or until a rich brown. Salt, of course.

OATMEAL GEMS.

Take one cup of oat-meal and soak it over night in one cup of water; in the morning add one cup of sour milk, one tea-spoon of saleratus, one cup of flour, a little salt. They are baked in irons as other gems and muffins. If on first trial you find them moist and sticky, add a little more flour, as some flour thickens more than others.

ROLLS.

Mrs. Hammond.

At *noon*, take two quarts of flour, and put into it one large tablespoonful of lard. Make a hole in the center and set it away. At night, take one cup of yeast, one half cup white sugar, and mix thoroughly with a pint of cold boiled milk. Add a little salt, and pour into the hole in the flour, and set away until morning, without stirring. Then with a stiff knife work in the flour, but do not knead. Let it set until it rises, then knead and roll out thin as doughnuts; cut out and fold together and set away to rise. Do not let the rolls touch when in the pan.

CINNAMON ROLLS.

Take a piece of pie crust, roll it out, cut it in narrow strips, sprinkle cinnamon over it, roll it up tight, put it in a clean tin pan, which has been well oiled with butter, brown nicely and bake. Then serve on the table.

FRENCH ROLLS.

Into one pound of flour rub two ounces of butter and the whites of three eggs, well beaten; add a tablespoonful of good yeast, a little salt, and milk enough to make a stiff dough; cover it and set it in a warm place till light, which will be an hour or more, according to the strength of the yeast. Cut into rolls, dip the edges into melted butter to keep them from sticking together, and bake in a quick oven.

OSCAR WILDE ROLLS.

Mrs. W. A. Hammond.

Two teacups raised dough, one-half teacup sugar, two tablespoonfuls butter, one egg. Mix thoroughly and roll out about an inch thick. Cut in strips about an inch wide. Commence at one end of a strip aud wind the strip round the center like a mat. Set them in a warm place for twenty minutes. Bake in a hot oven. About five minutes before they are done brush over the tips with sugar and water. Very good.

PARKER HOUSE ROLLS.

One pint scalded milk. Let it cool, and add two tablespoons sugar, two of lard, two of yeast, a little salt. In winter mix in batter over night, in morning knead; set to rise again, and at noon roll out very thin, cut in large rounds, put on a piece of butter and lay the dough over. Let it rise again, and bake for tea. In summer mix early in the morning instead of at night.

TEA ROLLS.

One tablespoon butter, one quart flour, two teaspoonsful baking powder, one-half teaspoon salt; milk to make a soft dough. Warm the butter, mix the baking powder into the flour, mix well together, aud then turn out on the board and knead to make it smooth; roll out one-half inch thick and cut with a large round cutter, then fold each one over to form a half-round, wetting a little between the folds to make them stick together; place them apart on the buttered pans, wash them over with milk so as to give them a gloss, and bake immediately in a hot oven twenty minutes.

RYE TEA CAKES.

One pint sweet milk, two eggs well beaten, one tablespoonful brown sugar, one-half a teaspoonful of salt; stir into this sufficient rye flour to make it stiff as common griddle-cake batter. Bake in gem pans one-half an hour. Serve hot.

TEA BISCUITS.

Two and one-half pounds flour, three ounces butter, two teaspoonsful baking powder, one pint milk, a pinch of salt. Rub butter, flour and baking powder; then add the milk, roll it out one inch thick, cut out, bake in hot oven.

HUCKLEBERRY CAKE.

Mrs. C. C. Fisher.

Two-thirds cup of sugar, one tablespoon of butter; cream the two together; two-thirds cup of milk, two cups of flour, one egg, two and one-half teaspoons of Horsford's baking powder, one pint of huckleberries (dry); rub the berries in flour to prevent settling.

RYE CAKES.

Mrs. Raymond, Boston.

1 cup of milk, one quarter cup of sugar, one half cup of butter (small), one egg, one pint rye meal, one teaspoonful of cream tartar, one half of soda.

RUSKS.

Take enough of light dough and work in a teacup of sugar and nearly as much shortening, mould out same as for light biscuit. Or, take a cupful of yeast, half a cup of lard or butter, a little soda; knead together, and when it rises mould out, and raise again before baking.

RUSKS.

Rusks reqnire a longer time for rising than ordinary rolls or biscuits. If wished for tea one evening, begin them the day before. In cold weather, to make up two and a half quarts of flour, mix into a paste with one pint of boiling water, two tablespoonfuls of sugar, three of flour, and two large Irish potatoes, boiled and mashed smooth. In the evening make up dough with this sponge, adding three well-beaten eggs, three-quarters of a pound of sugar, and half a pint of fresh milk. Set it away in a covered vessel, leaving plenty of room for it to swell. Next morning work into the risen dough, which should not be stiff, a quarter of a pound of butter and lard mixed. Make into rolls or biscuits, and let the dough rise for the second time. Flavor with two grated nutmegs or half an ounce of pounded stick cinnamon. When very light, bake in a quick, steady oven till of a pretty brown color; glaze with the yolk of an egg, and sprinkle lightly with powdered white sugar.

FRENCH TOAST.

Two-thirds of a pint of milk; one egg well beaten; a little salt. Take six slices of bread, dip into custard (uncooked) one by one; then fry in a little butter till a delicate brown. For sauce, melted sugar with a little cinnamon added. This is very nice, and a good way to use up stale bread. A good lunch dish.

CHEESE TOAST.

Melt new cheese in a buttered pan in a hot oven; when melted stir in mustard and cayenne pepper; pour over fried toast and serve.

RICH WAFFLES.

Make a thin paste with eight ounces of flour, six of pulverized sugar, two eggs, a few drops of essence to flavor, one-half a liquor glass of brandy or rum, and milk. Warm and butter both sides of the mold, put some of the paste into it; close it gently, set it on the fire, turn it over to heat both sides equally, dust them with sugar when done, and serve either warm or cold. It takes hardly a minute for each, with a good fire.

WAFFLES.

One pint of milk, three eggs beaten separately, two teaspoons baking powder, one tablespoon melted butter, a little salt, flour enough for a pretty stiff batter.

PASTRY, PIES.

"For nothing lovelier can be found in woman than to study household good, and good works in her husband to promote."—Milton.

One pound of sifted flour, one pound of fresh butter, two teaspoonfuls of cream of tartar, one teaspoonful of soda, a little water.

Work one-fourth of the butter into the flour until it is like sand; measure the cream of tartar and the soda, rub it through a sieve, put it to the flour, add enough cold water to bind it, and work it smooth; dredge flour over the pasteslab or board, rub a little flour over the rolling-pin, and roll the paste into about half an inch thickness, spread over the whole surface one-third of the remaining butter, then fold it up; dredge flour over the pasteslab and rolling-pin, and roll it out again, then put another portion of butter, and fold and roll again, and spread on the remaining butter, and fold and roll for the last time.

A LIGHT PUFF PASTE.

One pound butter, one pound flour, mix the flour with one-quarter of the butter, by rubbing it together and add enough cold water to make it the consistency of bread dough, roll this out to the thickness of one-half inch, put the balance of the butter on this in one lump and fold the four corners of the dough over the butter, entirely covering it, then roll it out to the thickness of one-quarter inch as nearly oblong as possible; then fold the ends over to the center until the sheet is about four inches wide; then roll it out again. Let it rest one-half hour each time and roll it out four times.

PUFF PASTE.

One cup cerealine, two cups butter, one teaspoon baking powder, one large cup of ice-water, three cups sifted flour, yolk of one egg, a little salt.

Sift the flour with the baking powder; place it on a pastry-slab or moulding-board, then add the cerealine, and mix thoroughly; form the whole into a ring, place the egg-yolk and salt in the center.

Add a little ice-water, and from the inside of the ring gradually take flour, and adding ice-water every time until you have a smooth, firm paste, very tenacious and lithe. Place it on ice for fifteen or twenty minutes, then roll out to the size of a dinner plate. Work the salt and buttermilk all out of the butter, and cut the butter in small pieces, and place on the dough. Work the edges of dough over the butter, carefully covering it. Turn it upside down, and roll it very thin; turn it back again, and fold into a three square. Repeat the rolling and folding three times.

Between each turn or operation of folding and rolling, put the dough on a thin tin on ice. As soon as it chills it will roll easily.

CHERRY PIE.

Choose fair ripe cherries, the large black English being the best for this purpose; wash and look them over carefully, fill the pie-plate evenly full, strew sugar over the top, dredge in plenty of flour, cover with a moderately thick upper crust, and bake one hour.

COCOANUT PIE.

Put a cup of cocoanut to soak in sweet milk as early in the morning as convenient. Take a teacup of the cocoanut and put it into a coffeecup, and fill up with milk. When ready to bake take two tablespoons of flour, mix with milk, and stir in three-fourths of a cup of milk (or water), place on the stove, and stir until it thickens. Add butter the size of a walnut while warm. When cool add a little salt, two eggs, saving out the white of one for the top. Sweeten to taste. Add the cocoanut, beating well. Fill the crust and bake. When done, have the extra white beaten ready to spread over the top. Return to the oven and brown lightly.

NO. 2.

Open the eyes of a cocoanut with a pointed knife or a gimlet, pour out the milk into a cup, then break the shell and take out the meat and grate it fine. Take the same weight of sugar and the grated nut and stir together; beat four eggs, the whites and yolks separately, to a stiff foam, mix one cup of cream and the milk of the cocoanut with the sugar and nut, then add the eggs and a few drops of orange or lemon extract. Line deep pie-tins with a nice crust, fill them with the custard, and bake carefully one-half an hour.

CUSTARD PIE.

Line your plate with pie crust, and fill it with a mixture of three eggs, one pint milk, one-half teacup of sugar, bake it in a medium hot oven, flavor with mace. For cocoanut pie, use the same custard as for custard pie, but put cocoanut in the plate before you pour the custard on it.

FRUIT PIE.

Line a soup plate with a rich paste, and spread with a layer of strawberry or raspberry preserves, over which sprinkle two tablespoons of finely chopped almonds (blanched of course), and one-half ounce of candied lemon peel cut into shreds. Then mix the following ingredients: One-half pound white sugar, one-fourth pound butter, melted, four yolks and two whites of eggs and a few drops of almond essence. Beat well together and pour the mixture into the soup plate over the preserves, etc. Bake in a moderately-warm oven. When cold sprinkle or sift a little powdered sugar over the top. A little cream eaten with it is a great addition.

LEMON PIE.

Mrs. McHenry.

Two lemons, rind of one grated, two tablespoons melted butter, four eggs, one and one-half cups sugar, three-fourths cup water, two tablespoons corn starch. Reserve for frosting whites of two eggs, three tablespoons sugar.

LEMON PIE.

Mrs. C. E. Elmes.

Yolks of two eggs, one cup of sugar, one and a half cups of water, one large lemon, three and one half tablespoons of flour. Line the pie-pan with crust and bake. Mix the flour with water, then add the other ingredients with it and boil it until it thickens, stirring constantly. Pour this mixture into the crust. Beat the whites of the eggs with half of the sugar and put on the top and brown in the oven.

LEMON CUSTARD PIE.

Mrs. J. R. Lyons.

One and one half cups water, two tablespoons cornstarch dissolved in a little cold water, and stirred into the water while boiling. The grated rind and juice of one large, or two small lemons; three eggs, save out whites of two for frosting, beat the remainder, with one cup of sugar, to a light cream; mix all thoroughly together, and when cold put into a crust, previously baked. Beat whites with a small tablespoon of sugar to each white, and spread over top. Brown in the oven.

ORANCE PIE.

Take the juice and rind of one orange; one small cup of sugar, yolks of three eggs, one tablespoon of corn-starch, made smooth with milk; piece of butter as large as a chestnut, and one cup of milk. Beat the whites of the three eggs with sugar, and place on the top after the pie is baked—leaving in the oven until browned.

ORANGE PIE, No. 2.

Take four good-sized oranges, peel, seed, and cut in very small pieces; add a cup of sugar and let stand; into a quart of nearly boiling milk stir two tablespoons of corn-starch mixed with a little water, and the yolks of three eggs. When this is done, let it cool, then mix with the oranges. Put it in simply a lower crust. Make a frosting of the whites of the eggs and one-half cup sugar. Spread it over top of pies, and place for a few seconds in the oven to brown.

ORANGE PIE No. 3.

Grate the rind of a large, sweet orange; squeeze the juice and press off the pulp, picking out the seeds. Cream one-fourth of a cup (or butter), one-half cup sugar, one egg beaten light, one tablespoon of flour rubbed smooth in one-half cup of water. Stir in the orange, and bake with two crusts. In this, as indeed in all cooking, judgment must be used, as oranges vary in size and sweetness; but these are the usual proportions, and are sufficient for an ordinary-sized pie.

PEACH AND APRICOT PIES.

Line your plate with pie crust, pare the fruit and lay it in the plate nicely sliced, fill the pie well, cover it with a piece of well greased paper and bake it. When done, put enough sugar on it to suit your taste. This pie will be nice if you beat four whites of eggs stiff and mix one-half cup powdered sugar in it; put this on top and bake it in a hot oven until it gets a little color.

LEMON PIE.

Juice and grated rind of one lemon, one cup of water, two tablespoons of corn-starch, one cup of sugar, one egg, a small piece of butter; boil the water, wet the corn-starch with a little cold water and stir it in; when it boils pour it over the sugar and butter; when cold, add the egg and lemon. Bake with two crusts.

MINCE MEAT.

Mrs. Wiswall.

Five and one-half pounds of meat before boiling, two and one-quarter pounds suet, two and one-half pounds stoned raisins, one and one-half pound currants, three-quarters of a pound of citron, small, thin pieces, two pounds brown sugar, one-half pint good molasses, one pint brandy (nearly a quart), one pint white wine (Madeira), one-quarter cup each of salt, cinnamon, allspice; one and one-half nutmeg, one-half tablespoon mace.

MINCE MEAT.

Three pounds meat (after it is boiled), four pounds suet, three and one-half pounds raisins, one and one-half pounds currants, one-half pound dried cherries, and mace to your taste. Four pints of white wine, one pint brandy, four pounds brown sugar.

MINCE MEAT.

Six cupfuls beef, twelve cupfuls apples, three cupfuls sugar, two cupfuls molasses, two cupfuls butter, two pounds raisins, one quart cider, three tablespoons cinnamon, two tablespoons all-spice.

CREAM RASPBERRY PIE.

Puff paste, one quart of raspberries, sugar to taste, a good teacup of milk, a pinch of soda, half a teaspoon of corn flour, one tablespoon of white pounded sugar, whites of two eggs. Line a pie-dish with puff paste, and fill with raspberries, sweetened to taste. Cover with pastry, but do not press this down at the edges; also rub the edge of the lower crust to prevent adhesion, and bake in a brisk oven. While it is cooking heat a small teacup of milk, with a pinch of soda in it, and stir into it the corn flour, which should be previously wetted with a little cold milk, add the white sugar, and cook for three minutes. pour the mixture into a small basin, and beat in the frothed whites of two eggs, whip to a cream, and let it get cold. When the pie is taken from the oven, lift the top crust and pour in the cream you have made, replace the crust and set aside to cool. Sprinkle a little sugar over the top before serving

PUMPKIN PIE.

Mrs. E. J. Hill.

Select a pumpkin that has a deep rich color, and firm, close texture. Stew and sift it. One large pumpkin will make fifteen pies. Allow two eggs to a pie, and three or four quarts of milk. To this quantity, two teaspoons ginger, four of cinnamon, twelve of allspice, two of cloves, and one nutmeg. Bake without cover in a good paste, quite slowly.

RHUBARB PIE.

Pare the rhubarb and cut it in small pieces, put in a sauce pan and cook it, applying a little sugar and sherry wine, for about ten minutes ; after it gets cold put it into the pie-dish and bake it. It will make a delicate pie if you just pare the rhubarb, cut it up, put it in the pie-dish, after being lined with pie crust, a good cup of sugar and cover it up with pie crust.

RHUBARB PIE.

Mrs. Ryer.

Cut the plant in small pieces, scald in boiling water about five minutes, and then take the pan off.

Add two cups of sugar, yolks of three eggs. Boil same as corn starch. Bake with one crust ; then cover tops with the whites of eggs well beaten. Bake again in hot oven about five minutes.

PUDDINGS, CUSTARDS, CREAMS, ETC.

GENUINE APPLE-DUMPLINGS.

The dumplings of our forefathers has been one of the neglected dishes of late years. The best way to make them, indeed the only old-fashioned "sure enough" way, is to pare and core very large apples, fill the hollow where the core is taken out with a little butter and sugar beaten together and flavored with nutmeg. Have ready some dough blankets made in the same way as tea biscuits, roll each apple in a blanket and join the edges by pinching them together. Then drop them into boiling water, cover them closely and boil steadily and uninterruptedly for about twenty minutes. The water must not stop boiling nor must the cover be removed until the dumplings are done. They should be served hot with hard sauce.

STEAMED APPLE DUMPLING.

Pare, core and slice thin four apples; make the paste of one tablespoon of butter, mixed in one pint of flour; two tablespoons baking powder, a little salt, and milk to form paste. Roll out and put the apples over the paste; roll up and steam two and one-half hours; eat with vanilla sauce.

APPLE FRITTERS.

Four eggs, two quarts of flour, two cups of sugar, one pint of currants, two teaspoons baking powder, three pints of milk, one teaspoon cinnamon, one teaspoon allspice, two quarts chopped apples; make in cone shapes, and fry in lard.

APPLE FRITTERS.

Mrs. H. H. Brown.

Pare and core the apples, and cut in slices about one-third of an inch thick; dip in the batter, and fry six minutes in boiling fat. Serve on a hot dish. Apples may be sprinkled with a little nutmeg, and let stand an hour before fried. Peaches, pears, pineapples, bannanas, etc., either fresh or canned, may be used for fritters.

FRITTER BATTER.

Mrs. H. H. Brown.

One pint of flour, half pint milk, one tablespoon of butter, one teaspoon of salt, two eggs. Beat the eggs light; add the milk and salt to them; pour half of this mixture on the flour, and when beaten light and smooth add the remainder of the butter; fry in boiling fat; sprinkle with sugar, and serve on hot dish. You can add two tablespoons of sugar to this batter when used with fruit.

BOILED APPLE TAPIOCA.

Mrs. Newell.

Wash and soak over night one large cup of tapioca; boil in a farina kettle until very clear, with just enough water to cover it. Before you put the tapioca on to boil, pare six large apples and slice into a stewpan, put on top of apples two lemons sliced, removing the seeds; put on this one large cup of sugar, and just enough water to keep the apples from burning; set pan on the back of the stove, cook slowly until very brown. When tapioca is good and clean, mix both apples and tapioca together and mash through a colander.

APPLE PUDDING.

Mrs. D. W. Coan.

Pare and slice enough sour apples to fill a round pudding dish holding a quart or little over; put two tablespoons of water into the dish with the apples; take two teaspoons sifted flour, two teaspoons baking powder, butter size of an egg; one egg beaten light, and enough sweet milk to mix the ingredients together into a very stiff batter; spread this over the apples evenly with a knife; bake in a moderate oven from one-half to three-fourths of an hour, and serve hot with cream and sugar, or any kind of sauce which is preferred. It may be steamed.

ENGLISH APPLE PUDDING.

Paste, take twelve or fourteen apples, peeled, cored and sliced, and one and one-half cups of sugar. Line an earthenware dish with the paste, pack in the apples, sugar and extract, wet the edges; cover, pinch the edges closely together; place in a saucepan half full of boiling water; flavor to suit your taste.

APPLE PLUM PUDDING.

Mrs. Ryer.

Five large apples, chopped; two cups of raisins, two cups of sugar, one cup of sweet milk, two cups of flour, two teaspoons baking powder, one-half cup butter, two eggs, pinch of salt; bake one hour. Serve with hard silver sauce.

APPLE SNOW PUDDING.

Take one-half pound of the pulp of soaked apples (seven or eight good sized), one-half pound granulated sugar, and the whites of two eggs; beat the latter to a stiff froth; then add a little of the sugar, then apple alternately, until the whole is mixed; continue the beating until light like a sponge. Make a rich custard, put into a dish and pile the snow on top. This makes a beautiful dish and is very palatable. One quart of milk will make enough for twelve persons.

BATTER PUDDING, BOILED.

Two cups of "cerealine," one cup of flour, one-half teaspoon of salt, one tablespoon of baking powder, two tablespoons of butter, one-half teaspoon of extract of lemon, three eggs, one pint of milk. Sift the flour, salt and baking powder together, add "cerealine;" eggs, well beaten; extract and milk; mix into the batter as for muffins; pour into a well-buttered mould; set in a saucepan with boiling water two-thirds up the sides of mould; steam one hour and serve with brandy sauce.

BARONESS PUDDING.

Three-quarters of a pound of suet, three-quarters of a pound of raisins, weighed after stoned, three-quarters of a pound of flour, one-half pint of milk, one-quarter saltspoon of salt. Prepare the suet by carefully freeing it from the skin, and chop it finely; stone the raisins, and cut them in halves, and mix both these ingredients with salt and flour; moisten the whole with the above proportion of milk, stir the mixture well, and tie the pudding in a floured cloth which has been previously wrung out in boiling water; put the pudding into a saucepan of boiling water, and boil it for four hours. Serve with sweet sauce.

BROWN BETTY.

A layer of bread crumbs in a pudding dish, then a layer of tart apples pared and cut in pieces half an inch thick, sprinkle over them a tablespoon of sugar and small pieces of butter (not too much). Continue this until the dish is full, having the bread crumbs on the top. Pour in half a teacup of water, and bake one hour. Serve with butter and sugar sauce, or eat with sugar and cream—nutmeg if you like.

CABINET PUDDING.

Mrs. H. L. H.

Use a perfectly smooth, plain mould. First butter the mould thickly with cold butter so that the fruit will stick. Arrange the fruit in wreaths, stars, leaves or any figures. Use rather dry fruit. French dried fruit make a nice pudding. Use half a pound of raisins, currants and citron for three pints. After the fruit is arranged, put on slices of cake, about quarter of an

inch thick, fitting it to the sides and bottom. Fill the mould with alternate layers of cake and fruit; pour in slowly a plain custard made of six eggs, four tablespoons of sugar, one teaspoon of lemon or vanilla extract. Mix the eggs and sugar, and add a pint of milk by heating two or three minutes. Steam the pudding by putting it in a pan half full of water and setting it in the oven. It will take about three-quarters of an hour to cook.

CHERRY PUDDING.

Mrs. H. H. Gregg.

One quart pitted cherries and juice, three-fourth box Cox's Gelatine, seven tablespoons of granulated sugar. Put all on the range and bring to a boil. Take off and cool a little. Add a wineglass of cherry or juice of one lemon; pour into a mould. When cold turn out on a plate, pour over all whipped cream.

CHOCOLATE PUDDING.

Mrs. Lovejoy.

One quart of milk, three tablespoons corn starch, one cup sugar, yolk of three eggs. three tablespoons grated chocolate, a little vanilla. Steam until stiff, then put on the meringue and brown slightly. Eat cold with cream and sugar.

COCOANUT PUDDING.

Soak one cup of cocoanut in milk. Rub one-half cup of butter with one cup of sugar, add three eggs, one cup of flour, a pinch of baking powder. and the cocoanut. Put this in a mould; set it in a pan of water; put both in an oven three to four hours.

COTTAGE PUDDING.

Mrs. C. C. Fisher.

One cup of sugar, butter the size of an egg, one-half cup of milk, two cups of flour, two teaspoons of baking powder, two eggs, vanilla flavoring. Sauce: One egg, one-half cup of sugar, one heaping teaspoon of corn starch, one pint of milk, flavor with vanilla.

(10)

DATE OR ANY FRUIT PUDDING.

Mrs. Lovejoy.

One-half pound dates, one-half pound bread crumbs, five ounces of suet, six ounces of white sugar, two eggs, a little salt, and nutmeg to taste. Steam three hours. If dates are used, make a warm sauce, and flavor with vanilla.

DELICATE PUDDING.

One cup granulated sugar, one cup sweet milk, one egg, butter size of an egg, one cup raisins, two teaspoons baking powder, flour to make consistency of cake, steam in greased basin one hour.

DELMONICO'S PUDDING.

Heat a quart of milk to nearly boiling, reserve a little to wet three tablespoons corn starch, beat up the yolk of five eggs, with six tablespoons sugar, stir these into the corn starch after being dissolved in the milk, then add to the hot milk, and boil three minutes; then add one teaspoon milk. Turn this into a buttered dish and bake ten minutes. Beat up whites, add three tablespoons white sugar, and one-half teaspoon vanilla. Spread on pudding and brown. Eat cold with cream sauce.

FAMILY STYLE PUDDING.

Line a mould with stale bread, put some layer raisins in and bread on top, and fill the mould this way. After the mould is filled, pour a little custard on it and let it soak one hour, then cover it up and set it in a slow oven about two or three hours.

ENGLISH PUDDING.

Mrs. F. M. Chisholm.

Three cups of flour, one cup of chopped suet, one cup of chopped raisins, one cup of milk, one cup of molasses, in which dissolve one teaspoon of soda, spice to taste. Steam four hours.

FIG PUDDING.

One-half pound of butter, one-half pound of figs cut small, one-half pound of bread crumbs, one-half pound of sugar, four eggs, a little grated nutmeg. Put the butter and figs in a saucepan, and simmer fifteen minutes; crumb the bread fine and mix it with the sugar, eggs and nutmeg in a basin, and pour the butter and figs over them; when lukewarm, mix all together. Butter a pudding mould and steam three hours. Serve with any nice hot sauce.

FIG PUDDING.

Mrs. H. H. Gregg.

One pound of figs soaked until soft and then chopped fine, two coffee cups of bread crumbs, one cup of brown sugar, three-fourths pound chopped suet, two eggs, and a little salt. Steam two hours.

FRITTERS.

Five cups of "Cerealine," one pint of milk, two tablespoons of sugar, a little mace, a little lemon extract, one tablespoon of butter, one-half teaspoon of salt. Mix thoroughly and cook for five minutes; set in a cold pan; when cold cut in pieces; dip into batter and fry, and serve with powdered sugar.

GRAHAM PUDDING.

Take a pint of water and allow it to boil thoroughly—not simmer—then salt, and stir in very slowly Graham flour—which must be fresh and sweet—until quite thick; after doing so, remove to the back part of the stove, and let it boil slowly for fifteen minutes or more; it must be stirred at intervals to prevent burning. Serve nearly cold, with syrup or sugar and cream.

INDIAN PUDDING.

Into a quart of boiling milk stir Indian meal enough to make a thick batter, with a tablespoon of butter; when cold add four eggs well beaten, a tablespoon of ginger, a teaspoon of salt, and one-half cup of syrup; mix well and bake three hours in a brown earthen dish, buttered.

BAKED INDIAN PUDDING.

For a two-quart pudding use two teacups meal; moisten the meal with cold water; then pour over it one pint of boiling water; add one tablespoon of butter, two teacups of sugar, one cup of raisins, three eggs well beaten before adding, and fill up with sweet milk; season with whatever spice is preferred; bake slowly one-half an hour or more.

BOILED INDIAN PUDDING.

One and one-half cups sour milk, two eggs well beaten, one small teaspoon saleratus dissolved in the milk; then sift in dry corn meal until of the consistency as if for griddle cakes (perhaps a little thicker); stir in a teacup of dried fruit—cherries are the best; put in a bag and boil one hour. For sauce, sweetened cream flavored with nutmeg.

LEMON PUDDING.

Mrs. Lovejoy.

One quart milk, two cups bread crumbs, one-half cup butter, one cup sugar, four eggs, one large lemon, juice and half the rind, grated; soak the bread in the milk, add the beaten yolks with the butter and sugar, rubbed to a cream, also the lemon. Bake in a buttered dish until firm, and slightly brown. Cover with the whites, a little sugar, and lemon juice. Brown slightly. Eat cold. An orange pudding may be made in the same way.

MOLASSES PUDDING.

Mrs. Willis Blackman.

Three cups of flour, one each of molasses, melted butter and hot water, one teaspoon of soda; steam three hours, serve with a sauce of butter and sugar worked to a cream, with hot water to make it the proper consistency, and flavor with vanilla. You can make a fruit pudding of it by adding a teacup of raisins and one of currants.

J. L. HATHAWAY,

ANTHRACITE AND BITUMINOUS

COAL,

38 MARKET STREET.

YARDS.

68 Kingsbury St.	Clybourn Place Bridge.
2423 S. Halsted St.	94 N. Wood Street.

CHICAGO, ILL.

TELEPHONE 837.

—THE—

CHICAGO CARPET CO.

Wabash Avenue, Cor. Madison Street,

—DEALERS IN—

Carpets, Furniture and Upholstery Goods,

AT LOWEST PRICES.

Estimates Given for Furnishing Churches, Hotels AND Residences Complete.

ORANGE PUDDING.

Cut after peeling, and put into a pudding dish, six juicy oranges, if small use seven, put on them one cup of sugar, make a smooth, thick custard with one pint of milk, the yolk of three eggs, and one tablespoon of corn starch. This should be stirred constantly while boiling, when done pour it on the oranges. Beat the whites to a stiff froth, add one tablespoon sugar and put on top of all. Put the dish in a pan of water in the oven long enough for it to brown on top. To be eaten cold. Can be made the day before it is wanted.

ENGLISH PLUM PUDDING.

Nine eggs beaten to a froth, add flour sufficient to make a thick batter free from lumps, add one pint new milk and beat well; add two pounds of raisins stoned, and two pounds currants washed and dried, one pound of citron sliced, one-fourth pound bitter almonds divided, three-fourths of a pound of brown sugar, one nutmeg, one teaspoon of allspice, mace and cinnamon, three-fourths of a pound beef suet, chopped fine; mix three days before cooking, and beat well again, add more milk if required. If made into two puddings boil four hours.

PLUM PUDDING.

One quart of flour, one coffee cup chopped raisins, one teacup of currants, one teacup chopped suet, one-half cup candied lemon finely shred, one cup brown sugar, one teaspoon of salt, two of baking powder, and two cups of sweet milk. Sift the flour, put in the baking powder and salt, mixing thoroughly. Next add the raisins, currants and candied lemons, and incorporate well with the flour, so they will not sink to the bottom, as they will always do unless mixed first with the flour. Then put in suet and sugar, and lastly the milk, and, after stirring well, put in a bag which has been dipped in boiling water, and boil three hours. Do not let the fire get low so the pudding will stop boiling, and replenish always from a boiling teakettle. When done, put on a large platter, remove the strings, and turn the bag wrong side out—that is, pull it gently back and it will come off smoothly, if the bag is well scalded. Omit the lemon if you do not care for it so rich. Sauce: One cup sugar, one-half cup butter, one tablespoon of flour, and one egg; melt the butter in the sauce-pan and stir in the flour until the whole is smooth, then stir in the egg, and pour upon this one pint of boiling water. By adding three tablespoons of brandy it becomes brandy sauce, or the juice and grated rind of a lemon, it is called lemon sauce.

PLUM PUDDING.

Mrs. Austin Wiswall.

Take ten soft crackers, pound them, put them into a quart of milk and let them stand over night. In the morning rub them through a colander. Beat up eight eggs, one pound of sugar, one cup molasses, one cup brandy, one pound suet, one tablespoon salt, one tablespoon nutmeg, one tablespoon mace, one-quarter pound citron cut in very small pieces, one pound currants, one and one-half pound stoned raisins, and half teaspoon cream of tartar, and one-fourth teaspoon soda, sifted into a scant tablespoon flour. Boil in a mould or cloth for five hours. Serve with a rich wine sauce. Sauce: Three cups sugar, one cup butter, and one-half tumbler wine, Madeira, poured hot over one egg, white and yolk beaten separately.

BAKED PLUM PUDDING.

Mix well in a large pan, half a pound of seedless fine raisins, the same quantity of currants, half a pound of bread crumbs, half a pint of boiling milk, half a pound of finely chopped suet, the yolks and whites of three well beaten eggs, a quarter of a pound of moist white sugar, an ounce of candied lemon, the same of orange and citron, half a grated nutmeg, with a small glass of brandy. Bake for one hour in a slow oven in a well buttered mould or dish.

PRUNE PUDDING.

Mrs. Boyles.

One pound prunes soaked over night, and stewed soft in a very little water. Take the stones out, and chop a little with a spoon, add two tablespoons of sugar, and the whites of four eggs, beaten very stiff, stir well together. Bake fifteen minutes. Sauce: One-half pint sweet whipped cream, and the white of one egg beaten stiff.

PRUNE PUDDING.

Miss K. A. Bishop.

Wash one pound of prunes, and soak over night with water enough to cover them; cook in the same water until very soft, take out the stones and rub through the colander to remove the large pieces of skin; heat again and when very thick add half a box of gelatine previously soaked in a little water, and a small teacup of sugar; take from the stove and add the well beaten whites of from three to five eggs (five making a much more delicious pudding). Serve cold wi h cream. It makes a very pretty dessert to put it in a glass dish, and put whipped cream upon it.

RAILROAD PUDDING.

One cup of molasses, one cup sweet milk, one cup suet, four cups of flour, one cup raisins, one cup currants (or all raisins); warm the molasses and stir in one teaspoon of soda; steam four hours. Flavor the sauce with nutmeg or currant jelly. If there is any left, it is just as good steamed over.

DELICIOUS RICE PUDDING.

Five pints of milk, one-half cup rice; put rice raw in the five pints of milk; sugar one and one-half cups, or to taste. Bake in an oven three or four hours.

TAPIOCA CREAM PUDDING.

Mrs. Lovejoy.

Cover three tablespoons of tapioca with water and let it stand over night. In the morning boil until clear in one quart of milk with a little salt; beat the yolks of three eggs, stir them in with one cup of sugar, and half a cocoanut grated; let it just boil, stirring all the time; put in a dish, spread the beaten whites and a little sugar on top, and brown it. Eat cold.

BOILED TAPIOCA PUDDING.

Soak until quite soft one cup of tapioca, then boil in milk enough to make it like jelly—perhaps fifteen minutes will suffice of steady boiling, constantly stirring; salt when put to soak. Pour out in moulds and eat with cream, sugar and currant jelly.

BAKED TAPIOCA PUDDING.

Soak eight tablespoons of tapioca in a quart of warm water or milk till soft; then add two tablespoons melted butter, five eggs well beaten, spice, sugar and wine to taste. Bake in buttered dish and without lining.

TAPIOCA PUDDING.

One cup of tapioca, one quart of milk, soak three hours on the back side of the stove; when soft, and if too thick, add more milk, then one-half cup of white sugar, the yolks of two eggs, small spoon of butter, a little salt and nutmeg. Bake slowly for an hour. Beat the whites of the eggs as frosting, and serve with pudding when done, or to be eaten as sauce, which I think is nicer than putting it on top of the pudding.

SAGO PUDDING.

Soak one cup of sago in warm water until it is swelled alike; add water as it thickens, keeping it warm on the back side of the stove; when all swelled peel six sour apples, core them, put them in the sago, sprinkle some sugar on top, bake until the apples are soft—say one-half an hour. To be eaten with cream and sugar.

SPONGE CAKE PUDDING.

Take three or four stale sponge biscuits, or as much stale sponge cake, and lay at the bottom of a well-buttered dish; beat well six eggs, and stir into them by degrees a pint and a half of boiling milk, three ounces of sugar, and a dessertspoon of grated lemon-peel; then add a tablespoon of brandy, pour the mixture over the cake, and let the pudding stand an hour. Then pour a little clarified butter over the top, cover it with sifted sugar, and bake three-quarters of an hour.

TRANSPARENT PUDDING.

Beat eight eggs very well, put them into a stew-pan with half a pound of fine-powdered sugar, half a pound of fresh butter, the grated outer rind of one lemon, and the juice of three. Stir it over the fire till it thickens, then pour it into a basin to cool. Line the edge of a buttered pudding-dish with thin puff-paste, pour in the pudding, and bake for three-quarters of an hour in a moderate oven. It is a clear, light pudding, very good cold or hot.

APPLE SAUCE.

Mrs. Jas. Smale.

Cook apples with very little water, and rub through a seive, then beat with an egg-beater, and when light, to pint and a half of sauce, add beaten whites of two eggs; put on ice. (Very good.)

DAINTY DESSERT.

Mrs. C. E. Crandall.

Grate a fresh cocoanut, beat whites of five eggs to stiff froth, add one pint thick sweet cream, and sweeten to taste. Beat together very light. Serve with cake and berries.

LEMON TARTS.

Line patty-pans with a rich crust, and bake (prick the bottom of the crust in each pan to let out the air), when done, fill with the recipe for lemon filling, and return to the oven for a few minutes.

CREAM TARTS.

Line patty-pans with a rich pie crust, prick them and bake, set them away until serving time. Just before you wish to eat them, whip some rich cream, have the bowl set on ice while whipping the cream, add a little powdered sugar and vanilla, and serve.

ALMOND CUSTARD.

Mrs. J. Anderson.

One pint of cream, one-fourth pound almonds (pounded to a paste), three eggs, yolks and whites beaten separately, one cup granulated sugar.

Scald the milk, add the yolk, the sugar, the almond paste, and finally the whites, and boil, stirring constantly till it thickens. When almost cold, pour into cups, make a meringue of the whites of three eggs, and three tablespoons powdered sugar, add any preferred extract, and heap upon each cup.

"Make custards and blanc manges in the Arnold Steam Cooker."

CONCORD CUSTARD.

One quart of milk, yolks of four eggs, three heaping tablespoons corn starch, half a cup of sugar, half teaspoon salt, small piece of butter, flavor to taste. Boil, and turn into a pudding dish. Beat the whites of the eggs to a stiff froth, add one tablespoon sugar, spread over the top, and brown in the oven. Serve cold with jelly or preserves.

RASPBERRY OR CURRANT CUSTARD.

Make a rich syrup of a pint of raspberry or currant juice, poured over eight ounces of loaf sugar. Skim it, and stir gradually into it, over a very slow fire, the well-beaten yolks of six eggs, and continue to stir for five or six minutes, then pour it out, and as it cools, stir in by degrees half a pint of cream, and a tablespoon of lemon juice. Serve in cups.

AN IMPORTANT RECIPE!

Read and Learn that the

ILLINOIS CLUB STABLES,

623 & 625 W. Madison St.,

Will furnish you with a fine Coupe or Brougham, drawn by one or two horses, instead of a Two-Wheeled Hansom Cab, at prices quoted below:

- All jobs of one hour or less.............$1.00
- All depots.............................. 1.00
- Waiting for delayed trains, half riding rates.
- To theaters and return.................. 2.00
- Calling and shopping, first hour, $1; each hour after............................ .75
- Pleasure riding, per hour............... 1.00
- Parties and return, West Side, not over a mile............................... 1.50
- Parties, one way......................... 1.00
- Parties and return, North Side, Chicago Avenue north; 12th street south.... 2.00
- Parties and return, South or North Side, North Avenue north; 23d st. south.. 2.50
- If kept waiting over 20 minutes in party work, charges will be made at the rate of 75c per hour.

We also keep on hand and at your service a large line of the finest Carriages at corresponding low rates.

Promptness, low prices and first-class accommodations are offered to secure and hold your trade. Let us hope to receive an early order.

TELEPHONE 7017.

LEMON CUSTARD.

Beat the yolks of eight eggs for half an hour to froth, and strain them, pour over them a pint of boiling water, and the outer rind of two lemons grated. Make the juice of two lemons into a syrup, with three ounces of sugar, and stir into the custard. Then set it over the fire, adding a glass of Madeira, and half a glass of brandy, and stir till it thickens. Pour it out and stir till cold, then serve in cups.

ORANGE CUSTARD.

Pour over six ounces of sugar in a pan, the juice of six oranges, and let it simmer to a syrup, then pour it out to cool. Beat up very well the yolks of six eggs, and mix with a pint of good cream. Set them over a slow fire, and stir continually till the custard thickens and begins to simmer. Mix the syrup gradually, and stir a few minutes longer, then turn out and stir till cold, when it can be transferred to the custard-dish or cups.

GOOD CUSTARD.

Put into a sauce-pan a pint of milk and a pint of cream, with a stick of cinnamon, two peach-leaves, and the thin rind of half a lemon, and let it simmer half an hour. Then strain and put on again with three ounces of sugar. Beat very well the yolks of six eggs, and mix gradually with the milk, stirring continually over the fire with a wooden spoon till it thickens, but do not allow it to boil. Pour it out and add a glass of brandy, continuing to stir it till cool; then fill the custard cups and serve.

A FLOATING ISLAND.

Half fill a dish with rich custard; then place in the center a round slice of stale sponge cake, covered with any red jelly, then a smaller round of cake, each smaller than the last, and sweetmeats of varied colors, till you form a pyramid. Whip sweetened cream for the summit.

IRISH MOSS.

Soak a scant handful of Irish moss in strong soda-water until it swells, then spueeze the moss until it is free from water, and put it in a tin bucket which contains six pints of sweet milk. Set the bucket in a large iron pot which holds several pints of hot water; stir seldom, and let it remain until it will jell slightly by dropping on a cold plate. Strain through a sieve, sweeten and flavor to taste. Rinse a mould or a crock with tepid water, pour in the mixture, and set it away to cool. In a few hours it will be palatable. Eat with cream and sugar—some add jelly.

ARROW ROOT JELLY.

Mrs. Brown.

One pint water, one lemon, three spoons arrow root; slice the lemon in the water, let it scald; then strain, braid the arrow root with cold water, then stir in, adding a little salt; let it boil five minutes. This is especially nice in sickness.

LEMON JELLY.

Miss Bishop.

Pour on one-half a box of Cox's gelatine two-thirds of a pint of cold water, and let it stand about one-half an hour; then add two cups of sugar, three of boiling water; the juice and rind of four lemons. Strain and set upon ice. Use this same recipe for wine jelly, with one cup of wine, and leaving out the lemon if desired.

WINE JELLY.

Mrs. H. H. Brown.

One box of gelatine, one quart of boiling water; let it stand until dissolved, stirring occasionally. One pint of sugar, one pint of wine (Sherry), juice of three fresh lemons, and rind of two; mix well, and strain through a sieve. This will keep several days.

WINE JELLY, No. 2.

One box of gelatine one pint cold water; let it stand twenty minutes; juice and rind of two lemons, two cups of sugar, one pint of cider (hard is preferred), strain through a muslin bag. This makes three pints of jelly.

WINE SAUCE.

One-half pound butter, yolks of two eggs, beaten well and creamed with butter; nine tablespoons nice brown sugar, two glasses of wine. Let it simmer on the fire a short time.

FRENCH SAUCE.

Cream half a pound of butter, and stir in half a pound of sugar; then add the yolk of an egg and a gill of wine. Put it on the fire, stir till it simmers.

A NICE SAUCE FOR PUDDINGS.

Half a pound of butter, eight tablespoons brown sugar, and the white of one egg. The butter must be creamed and the sugar beaten into it, then the eggs; the wine poured gently in and stirred till the sauce is cold, then add the extract of nutmeg, Make it in a common sauce tureen, stirring all the while. Do not let it boil. Flavor with lemon or vanilla.

PUDDING SAUCE.

Mrs. C. E. Crandall.

One cup white sugar, one-half cup butter, beat together to cream, add one egg beaten very light. Beat together with egg-beater five minutes. Flavor.

A DELICIOUS BROWN SAUCE.

One-half pint of milk, one tablespoon of butter, two tablespoons of flour, and two tablespoons of molasses. Boil ten minutes.

A FINE FLAVORING.

Miss Lovejoy.

Orange rind grated and covered with alcohol, and set aside for some months.

LEMON MERINGUE.

Take one large sponge cake sliced, one quart of milk, three eggs, whites and yolks separate, five large tablespoons of pounded white sugar, two tablespoons of extract of lemon, and one-quarter of the rind of a lemon finely grated. Slice the cake and arrange it in a deep glass dish, then pour upon it a teacup of hot milk to soak it. Beat the yolks of the eggs, and stir with them four tablespoons of sugar; heat the rest of the milk, and pour it upon the eggs by degrees, stirring all the time; return it to the saucepan, and continue stirring until it thickens; let it cool a little, add the flavoring and pour over the sponge cake. When perfectly cool, heap upon it a meringue made of the whites of the eggs, whipped to a stiff froth, sweetened with the other tablespoon of sugar, and flavored with extract of lemon and rind. The meringue should be made just before serving.

MERINGUES.

One cup of granulated sugar to the whites of three eggs. Beat the eggs very stiff, mix a few drops of vanilla in the sugar, mix the sugar and eggs together as lightly as possible, then drop on buttered paper; cool oven so that they will dry before they will brown, and leave in the oven until they are dried. Then open the drafts to make the oven hotter so they will brown a little. Take one pint of cream, beat until stiff, put two meringues together like lady fingers with whipped cream between. Makes a delicious dessert.

A BEAUTIFUL DESSERT.

Five small tablespoons of corn starch, four tablespoons of sugar, four tablespoons of grated chocolate, one quart of milk. Put the milk on the stove and while it is heating mix the rest of the ingredients in a bowl with a little cold milk; then pour into the hot milk and boil a few minutes until it thickens; pour into a mould and set aside to cool. Make a boiled custard of one quart of milk, five eggs, leaving out the whites of two; two tablespoons of sugar. When the pudding is cold turn it into a shallow glass dish or platter, and pour the custard, which must be cold, around it, leaving the pudding two or three inches out of the custard. Take the whites of the eggs beaten to a stiff froth with two tablespoons of pulverized sugar, drop from a spoon about the size of kisses over the pudding and custard. Part of the eggs can be colored with cochineal syrup, and a small drop put on each kiss.

LEMON HONEYCOMB.

Put into a dish the juice of a good-sized lemon with two ounces of powdered sugar; whisk the white of one egg, a pint of cream, and an ounce of sifted sugar into stiff froth; skim it off as it foams, and lay it upon the lemon-juice till all of the cream is exhausted. Let it stand a day before you serve it. This is a cheap and pretty dish.

MARYLAND FLOAT.

Mrs. W. A. H.

Whites of four eggs beaten to a stiff froth, half a tumbler of jelly or jam, one cup of fine white sugar. Stir the sugar and jelly together thoroughly, and then add the whites of the eggs gradually, beating all together. Eaten with cream. Apple sauce will do.

BANANNA SOUFFLE.

Cut fine banaunas into slices lengthwise, as thick as a dollar; arrange them on a dish so that the ends of the long semi-circle slices meet and form a hollow centre. Pour over them a gill of sherry made very sweet with sugar and with which you have put one teaspoon of lemon juice; let them get ice cold, then fill the centre with whipped cream, piled high. This is delicious.

OMELET SOUFFLE.

Six whites and the yolks of three eggs, three ounces of pulverized sugar, and a flavoring of lemon or vanilla. First beat the yolks and sugar to a light cream, and add a few drops of flavoring, then beat the whites to the stiffest possible froth. Have the yolks in a deep bowl, turn the whites over them and mix them carefully with a rotary motion. Turn them into a baking dish two or three inches deep, slightly buttered; smooth over the top, sprinkle over sugar, and put into a moderate oven. When it has risen well and is of a fine yellow color, it is ready to be served. It should be eaten at once, or it will fall.

LEMON BUTTER.

Juice of six fine lemons, rind of two beaten with the yolk of three eggs, one tablespoon butter, three cups sugar. Boil in a dish set in hot water until it thickens,

CAKES, ETC.

"Open thy mind to that which I reveal, and fix it there within; for 'tis not knowledge, the having heard without retaining it."

—Dante.

MEASURES AND WEIGHTS.

One pint of sifted flour is one pound.
One pint of white sugar is one pound.
One tablespoon dry material is one ounce.
Two tablespoons liquid is one ounce.

ANGEL CAKE.

Miss Helen Hill.

The whites of twelve eggs, one tumbler of flour, one and one-half tumblers of sugar, one small spoon of cream tartar, pinch of salt. Sift flour and sugar separately and together five times. Beat eggs to a stiff froth. Bake forty minutes in moderate oven. Make thin lemon icing for the top. No flavoring in cake.

ANGEL CAKE.

Mrs. Raymond.

The whites of eleven eggs, one and one-half cups of granulated sugar sifted, one cup of flour sifted three times; then add one teaspoon of cream tartar to flour and sift again; one small teaspoon of vanilla.

ANGEL CAKE.

From Horsford's Cook Book.

Take one cup flour and put into it one heaping teaspoon Horsford's baking powder, sift the whole four times. Beat the whites of eleven eggs to a stiff froth, and then beat in one and one-half cups sugar and a teaspoon vanilla. Add the flour and beat lightly but thoroughly. Bake in an ungreased pan, slowly, forty minutes. When done turn it over to cool; place something under the corner of the pan so that the air will circulate underneath and assist the cooling. Cut it out when cool.

ALMOND CAKE.

Horsford's Cook Book.

Blanch and pound in a mortar eight ounces of sweet and one ounce of bitter almonds; add a few drops of rose-water or white of egg every few minutes to prevent oiling, add six tablespoons of sifted sugar and eight beaten eggs, sift in six tablespoons of flour, and work it thoroughly with the mixture. Gradually add a quarter of a pound of creamed butter, beat the mixture constantly while preparing the cake or it will be heavy, add two teaspoons Horsford's baking powder. Put a buttered paper inside of a buttered tin, pour in the mixture, and bake in a quick oven. Cover the cake with paper if the oven is too hot.

MRS. ECKARDT'S ALMOND CAKE.

Ten eggs, one and one-half pounds sugar, one-fourth pound grated chocolate, one-fourth pound choppel almonds, five ounces citron, one teaspoon cinnamon, one teaspoon cloves, one soup-plate grated white bread. Beat the yolks very light with the sugar half an hour, then add almonds and other ingredients. At last beat whites to a very stiff froth, and then bread crumbs, three tablespoons of brandy. Bake in medium oven. When baked spread jelly between layers. Ice with almond icing.

BLACK CAKE.

One pint molasses, one pint brown sugar, one pint of butter, one pint sour milk, three eggs, two teaspoons soda, cloves, nutmeg, cinnamon, one pound raisins. Make it very stiff, and bake in a slow oven. This will make two large cakes.

BLACK FRUIT CAKE.

Mrs. E. J. Hill.

One pound brown flour, one pound brown sugar, one pound citron, two pounds currants, three pounds stoned raisins, three-fourths pound of butter, one teacup of molasses, two teaspoons mace, two teaspoons cinnamon, one teaspoon cloves, one teaspoon soda, twelve eggs. This is an excellent recipe, and will make two large loaves. It will keep a year (if locked up.)

CARAMEL CAKE.

Mrs. A. D. Smith.

One and one-half cups of sugar, one-half cup of butter, one cup of milk, two cups of flour, three eggs beaten separately, one and one-half teaspoons of Horsford's baking powder, one teaspoon vanilla. Frosting: Two-thirds cup of milk, two cups of sugar, piece of butter size of an egg. Boil ten minutes and beat until cold. Flavor with vanilla. The cake makes three layers on a good-sized jelly tin, put the frosting between the layers, and on top.

CHOCOLATE CAKE.

Mrs. C. L. Gould.

Beat one cup sugar and one-half cup butter to a cream, add one cup milk, and add two cups of flour with three teaspoons of Horsford's baking powder mixed in the flour. Mix well, flavor and add whites of four eggs, beaten stiff. This is good for any large cake.

CHOCOLATE FROSTING.

One-fourth cake Baker's chocolate grated; melt it and add three tablespoons of milk, yolks of two eggs; thicken with confectioner's sugar; flavor with vanilla.

CHOCOLATE CAKE.

Mrs. O. L. Fox.

Two cups sugar, one cup butter, one cup sour milk, five eggs, three cups flour, one teaspoon soda, two teaspoons of vanilla, one-fourth cake of chocolate grated. Beat butter and sugar to cream, add the yolks of eggs beaten. Heat the milk and chocolate enough to melt it, add soda and beat with the butter and sugar; add the flour and vanilla, and last the whites beaten stiff.

CITRON CAKE.

Four eggs well beaten, one and one-half pounds sugar, three-fourths pound butter, one pint sweet milk, one and one-half pounds of flour, one-half pound citron. Cut in thin pieces well floured; two teaspoons Horsford's baking powder.

CREAM CAKE.

Three eggs, one cup of sugar, one-half cup of boiling water, two cups of flour, two teaspoons of Horsford's baking powder. Beat the sugar and eggs well together, then add the boiling water, and then the flour, to which has been added the baking powder; bake in three layers for about twenty minutes. Vanilla flavoring.

CREAM FOR FILLING.

One tablespoon of corn starch wet in a little milk, one cup of milk, one egg, sugar to taste. Put the milk in a basin to boil; as soon as it boils pour in the corn starch which has been dissolved in a little milk, let it boil about two minutes; then remove it from the stove, sweeten to taste with sugar, and flavor with vanilla.

CREAM CAKES.

One pint of milk, a little salt. Let it come to a scald, then stir in flour (which has been sifted three times) slowly until thick enough to mould; six eggs stirred in without beating, one by one, then drop into hot lard, fry brown; sand with pulverized sugar, to be sprinkled on while hot. A little spice if you like, mixed with the sugar.

CREAM CAKE.

Two tablespoons butter, two teacups sugar, three eggs, one-half teacup sweet milk, two tablespoons cold water, two teacups flour, two teaspoons of Horsford's baking powder; bake quickly on three or four round tins. The "cream" for same is one-half pint milk, one-half teacup sugar, small piece of butter, one egg,

one tablespoon of corn starch. Boil until very thick; when nearly cold flavor with vanilla. When the cakes are cool, put them together with it.

CUP CAKES.

One-half pound butter, three-quarters pound sugar, five eggs, one cup of milk, one-half pound flour, one spoonful Horsford's baking powder. Rub the sugar and butter well, then add eggs, milk and flour last: fill this in small round mould and bake quick.

DELICATE CAKE.

Whites of four eggs, one cup of milk—very full, one-half cup butter, two cups sugar, two and one-half cups flour, heaping teaspoon Horsford's baking powder. This makes two loaves. If you want it *very* nice, use one cup of corn starch in place of one of flour.

COMMON DARK CAKE.

Mrs. Raymond, Boston.

One heaping cup butter, two cups of sugar, one cup molasses, one large cup of milk, five eggs, teaspoon of soda, one teaspoon of each kind of spice, four and one-half cups of flour, currants, raisins and citron.

DROP CAKES.

One pint flour, one cup butter, one cup of sugar, four eggs, one-half cup of milk, one teaspoon of soda, two teaspoons cream tartar. Drop in tins. They are very nice if eaten when fresh.

EXCELSIOR SUGAR GINGERBREAD.

One and one-half cups of butter, three cups of sugar, one-half cup of sweet milk, with two-thirds teaspoon of soda, three teaspoons of yellow ginger, two eggs, flour enough to roll out very thin. Cut in squares, and bake twenty minutes. Sprinkle a little sugar over before baking.

FIG CAKE.

Mrs. Dr. Leroy.

One cup of butter, two cups of sugar, three and one-half cups of flour, one-half cup of milk, whites of two eggs, two teaspoons Horsford's baking powder. Bake in layers.

Filling. One pound of figs chopped fine, put in a stew-pan, pour over it one teacup of water; add one-half cup of sugar. Cook until soft and smooth. Let it cool and spread between the layers.

FIG CAKE.

Mrs. Willis Blackman.

Silver part. Two cups of sugar, two-thirds of a cup of butter, two-thirds of a cup of sweet milk, white of eight eggs, three heaping teaspoons of Horsford's baking powder, thoroughly sifted with three cups of flour, stir sugar and butter to a cream, add milk, flour, and, lastly, whites of eggs. Bake in two layer cake pans.

Gold part. One cup of sugar, three-fourths cup of butter, half cup of sour milk, one and one-half teaspoons of baking powder sifted in a little more than one and a half cups of flour, yolks of seven, and one whole egg thoroughly beaten, one teaspoon allspice and cinnamon. Put half of the cake in a layer cake pan, and lay on one pound halved figs (sifted over with flour) so that they will just touch each other; put on the rest of the gold part and bake. Put the cakes together with frosting while warm, the gold between the white ones, and cover with frosting.

FRENCH LOAF.

One pound of flour, one pound of sugar, three-quarters of a pound of butter, one pound of raisins, one-half pound of currants, eight eggs, one-half teaspoon of baking powder, one lemon juice and rind, one wine glass of wine, one nutmeg. Stir butter and sugar together, then add the lemon, the yolks, fruit, wine, nutmeg, and the whites beaten very light. Lastly add the flour. Stir as little as possible after it is all together.

SOFT GINGER CAKE.

Mrs. Dr. Leroy.

One cup sugar, two-thirds cup butter, one cup New Orleans molasses, heaping teaspoon soda put into the molasses, one teaspoon ginger, three and a half cups of flour, cup of milk, two eggs, pinch of salt. *Stir well ten minutes.*

GOLD AND SILVER CAKE.

One teacup white sugar, one-half teacup butter, whites of four eggs, two-thirds teacup sweet milk, two teacups flour, two teaspoons Horsford's baking powder; flavor.

GOLD CAKE.—Same as above, using the yolks of the four eggs, and adding one whole egg.

ICELAND WHITE FRUIT LOAF.

Horsford's Cook Book.

The whites of twelve eggs, two cups powdered sugar, one cup sweet cream, one-fourth cup brandy, one quart flour, two tablespoons Horsford's baking powder, two pounds chopped almonds, two cups of cut citron, two cups grated cocoanut, two teaspoons lemon extract. Bake until thoroughly done, in a moderately hot oven.

ICE CREAM CAKE.

Mrs. J. E Montrose.

This is an elegant cake. One cup butter, two cups sugar, two cups flour, one cup corn starch, one cup sweet milk, whites of eight eggs, two large teaspoons Horsford's baking powder.

FROSTING.—Four cups sugar, one pint boiling water, cook until it looks like candy; beat whites of four eggs, pour the sugar over all, stirring all of the time; dissolve a lump of citric acid in a little cold water, then put a teaspoon of acid in icing.

JELLY CAKE.

One pound powdered sugar, one pound flour, twelve eggs, separate the white from the yolk and beat the whites to a stiff foam, then put the sugar in and stir it a little, put in the yolks and the flour, mix lightly, put it in a pieplate and bake it; then fill the sheets with jelly and ice the top of the cake with a mixture of ornamenting sugar and water.

ROLL JELLY CAKE.

Mrs. Dr. Leroy.

One-half cup sugar, one and one-half cups flour, five eggs, whites and yolks beaten separately, three-fourths teaspoon of Horsford's baking powder, pinch of salt. This makes three thin cakes baked on long biscuit tins. While warm put jelly on under side and roll. Roll in clean wrapping paper and tie with a string to keep it in shape.

LOAF CAKE.

Mrs. D. W. Coan.

Four pounds flour, two and one-half pounds sugar, two pounds shortening, two-thirds butter and one-third lard; one quart milk, five eggs, one-half ounce nutmeg, one-half goblet wine, one cake yeast, two and one-half pounds raisins. Mix butter and sugar to cream. Take half of this and mix with the flour and milk warmed, and yeast and let it stand until light. Then mix in the rest of the ingredients, let it rise and bake.

MARBLE CAKE.

Light part: One cup butter, three cups of sugar, one-half cup of cream or milk, whites of seven eggs, two teaspoons of cream tartar, one of soda, and three and one-half cups of flour.

Dark part: One cup of butter, two of brown sugar, one of molasses, two tablespoons of cinnamon, one of cloves and allspice, one of nutmeg, one-half cup of cream or milk, one-half teaspoon of soda, yolks of seven eggs, five cups of flour. Butter your pan and put in a layer of dark, then a tablespoon of light, and alternate until all is used.

MARBLE CAKE.

Mrs. C. E. Crandall.

White part: One cup pulverized sugar, one-half cup butter, one-half cup sweet milk, whites of four eggs beaten stiff, two and one-half cups flour, two heaping teaspoons baking powder. Flavor.

The "Chicago Cottage" Gas Range

A Departure in Gas Cooking Stoves.

WE WILL GUARANTEE THE OVEN IN THIS RANGE

TO BAKE
Bread, biscuit, pies, cakes, etc., perfectly, browning the top delicately and beautifully, and more quickly than any other oven.

TO ROAST
Meats; cooking them as thoroughly as may be desired, without drying up the juices as in many other ovens.

TO BAKE AND ROAST AT THE SAME TIME
without one article tasting of the other in the slightest degree.

TO TOAST AND BROIL
quickly and thoroughly, without producing smoke.

Send for Catalogue, or call on

Telephone No. 5687. **CHICAGO GAS STOVE CO., Manufacturers,**
117 & 119 Lake St., CHICAGO, ILL.

GRIFFIN'S

WEST END STEAM CARPET CLEANING

AND BEATING WORKS.

Lace Curtains Laundried equal to new.

849 AND 851 WEST MADISON ST., CHICAGO.

Good Work and Reasonable Prices. Work Called for and Delivered to any part of the City.

TELEPHONE 7181. **G. W. GRIFFIN, PROP'R.**

FRED CROKER,

MERCHANT TAILOR,

CLEANING, DYEING AND REPAIRING.

117 South Western Avenue, - CHICAGO.

ORDERS BY POSTAL PROMPTLY ATTENDED TO.

Dark part: One cup brown sugar, one-half cup molasses, one-half cup sour milk, two and one-half cups flour, one teaspoon soda in milk and molasses; yolks of four eggs, one-half cup butter rubbed with the sugar, one-half teaspoon cinnamon, allspice and cloves.

MARBLE CAKE.

Horsford's Cook Book.

For the white portion: Take one cup of butter, three of white sugar, one of sweet milk, five of flour, one and one-half teaspoons Horsford's baking powder and the whites of eight eggs; mix properly, flavoring with lemon.

For the colored portion: One cup butter, three of brown sugar, one of molasses, one of sweet milk, four of flour, three teaspoons Horsford's baking powder, the yolks of eight eggs and one whole egg; mix properly and flavor with cinnamon, nutmegs and cloves. Put into the pans first a layer of the dark part, and then a layer of the white part, and alternate thus until the pans are as full as you may desire. Let the last layer be dark. This is a very nice and good-looking cake.

MOCK LADY CAKE.

Mrs. Dr. Leroy.

One-half cup of butter, two cups sugar, one cup milk, whites of four eggs, one-half teaspoon of soda, one teaspoon cream of tartar, three cups of flour, flavor as you please.

MOLASSES DROP CAKE.

One cup of molasses, three cups of flour, half a cup of butter, two teaspoons of extract of lemon, and one teaspoon of soda. Beat the ingredients together thoroughly, and drop in spoonfuls upon a buttered tin. Bake five or six minutes.

MOONSHINES.

One quart of flour, one tablespoon of butter, one teaspoon of salt, one tumbler of ice water. Mix all together with a knife. Place on a moulding board as for paste, beat with the rolling-pin until perfectly smooth and flexible. Roll thin as a wafer, cut in rounds and bake in a flat tin.

ORANGE CAKE.

Mrs. Raymond.

The yolk of five eggs beaten well, two cups of sugar, one-half cup of cold water, the juice and rind of one orange, one teaspoon of soda, two of cream tartar, two cups of flour, last of all the whites of three eggs beaten to a stiff froth.

FROSTING: The whites of two eggs and three cups of powdered sugar, the juice and rind of two oranges. Do not beat the whites for frosting. Split the cake and put between as well as on top. Bake in two sheets. (Very nice).

NUT CAKE.

Two cups of sugar, one of butter. three of flour, one of cold water, four eggs, three teaspoons of Horsford's baking powder, one and one-half cups kernels of hickory or white walnuts.

NUT CAKE.

One cup butter, two of white sugar, four of flour, four of sweet-milk, the whites of eight eggs, three teaspoons of Horsford's baking powder. two cups, hickory nuts picked out of the shell and cut up with a clean knife.

POUND CAKE.

One pound butter, one pound sugar, one pound flour, nine eggs beaten separately. one tablespoon of cream, one small glass brandy, a little nutmeg. Use either stoned raisins or currants.

RAISIN CAKE.

Cup of sugar, half cup of butter; add two eggs, two and a third cups of flour, one teaspoon of cream of tartar, one-half teaspoon of soda dissolved in a half cup of water, cup of chopped raisins, teaspoon of extract of lemon.

RIBBON CAKE.

Horsford's Cook Book.

Two and one-half cups of sugar, two and one-half cups of flour into which has been sifted two heaping teaspoons Horsford's baking powder, one cup butter, one cup sweet milk, and four eggs; divide into three parts. To one part add one cup raisins and one cup currants, spice to taste and bake. Then put the part with the fruit between the other two, spreading a very thin layer of jelly between. Frosting may be added if desired.

SPICE CAKE.

Mrs. Rugg.

One cup molasses, one cup sugar, two-thirds cup butter, one cup sour milk, three eggs, one teaspoon soda, one teaspoon nutmeg, one and one-half teaspoons cinnamon, one teaspoon cloves, three cups flour.

SPONGE CAKE.

Mrs. Raymond.

One-half pound sugar, five eggs, one-fourth pound flour, lemon juice.

ENGLISH WALNUT CAKE.

One cup butter, two cups sugar, one cup milk with one-half teaspoon soda. one teaspoon cream tartar, three and one-half cups flour, five eggs, one pound walnuts, leaving out a few to put on the frosting with the whites of two eggs.

WALNUT CAKE.

Mrs. S. M. Caligar.

Three eggs; beat them two minutes; one-half cup sugar, beat five minutes; one cup cold water, two teaspoons Horsford's baking powder, two and one-half cups flour.

Filling: Three cups sugar, three-fourths cup boiling water, —boil till crystalized, add whites of three eggs, beat to a froth. Beat until stone cold; then add one spoonful vanilla. Bake in layers, spread frosting on each layer, sprinkle each with the broken nuts, decorate the top with half nuts.

WASHINGTON AMBROSIA.

Mrs. Mortimer.

Two cups sugar, one-half cup butter, three cups flour, seven eggs beaten separately, one-half cup sweet milk, three teaspoons Horsford's baking powder. Make in layers.

Filling: Make a whiting of four or five eggs, and add the juice and pulp of two oranges, and one-half the grated pulp of one, beat or mix with the whiting and spread between layers. The above will make two cakes of three layers each.

A VERY NICE WEDDING CAKE.

Mrs. Raymond, Boston.

One-fourth pound butter, one and one-half pounds of flour, one and one-half dozen eggs, leaving out one-half of the whites for frosting. One cup molasses, one dessert spoon of soda, two large tablespoons of nutmeg, two also of allspice, two and one-half of cloves, three and three-fourths of cinnamon, not quite a heaping one of mace, two wine glasses of brandy, one of wine, currants four and one-half pounds, also of raisins, citron, one pound. This makes two very large, or four small ones.

WHITE CAKE.

Mrs. Mortimer.

One cup sugar, one-half cup butter, one-half cup sweet milk, whites of five eggs, two and one-half cups flour, two small spoons of Horsford's baking powder, extract of lemon. Can be baked plain or in layers with custard, cocoanut or anything between. For the custard take yolks of four eggs, one table-spoon sugar, one-half pint milk; flavor with vanilla.

WHITE AND FRUIT CAKE.

Mrs. Mortimer.

Whites of six eggs, three cups flour, one cup butter, one cup sweet milk, two cups sugar, two teaspoons of Horsford's baking powder; mix and divide into two parts; bake one-half in two pans; add to the other half one teaspoon ground cinnamon, one-half teaspoon ground cloves, one tablespoon molasses, two tablespoons whisky, one small cup cut raisins, and a little citron. Bake in two layers and pile alternately with the white cake, spreading jelly between.

COOKIES.

Mrs. A. D. Smith.

One cup butter, one cup sugar, three eggs well beaten, one teaspoon very full of Horsford's baking powder. flour enough to roll out. Flavor to taste.

SOFT GINGER COOKIES.

Two teacups New Orleans molasses, one teacup of melted lard, one teacup of boiling water, four teaspoons of soda bought in bulk, one teaspoon of ginger. Pour the boiling water on the soda. Do not knead too stiff. Bake with steady heat.

GINGER COOKIES.

Mrs. Newell.

One cup molasses, one cup sugar, one cup butter, one teaspoon soda dissolved in boiling water, one tablespoon ginger. Flour to make stiff. roll thin and bake quickly.

GINGER COOKIES.

Mrs. Nathan Farwell.

One cup sugar, one cup molasses, one cup butter, one cup sour milk, two eggs, two teaspoons soda, cinnamon and ginger. Wash the tops with beaten eggs. Roll, as soft as possible. half an inch thick.

SUGAR COOKIES.

Mrs. Ryer.

Two cups of sugar, one cup of butter, one-half cup of sour cream. one-half nutmeg, three eggs, one scant teaspoon soda. Mix as soft as possible.

CREAM PUFFS.

Mrs. Dr. Leroy.

Boil together one pint of milk, three-fourths cup of butter. When boiling add two even cups dry flour. When cool add six eggs well beaten. Drop on a buttered tin from a spoon. Bake about one-half hour in a hot oven. It is necessary to have a bright tin. Make them small.

Cream for filling. Boil one pint of milk (add two eggs, one cup of sugar, one cup of flour beaten together), one teaspoon vanilla and a little butter. Cut a hole in the side of each puff and fill with the cream.

CRULLERS.

Mrs. D. N. Conn.

One cup milk, two eggs, one and one-half cups sugar, two tablespoons butter, nutmeg, a little salt, two teaspoons Horsford's baking powder. Stir in flour till it is stiff enough to roll. Fry in lard.

CRULLERS.

One pint milk, one pint sugar, four eggs, one-half cup butter, two quarts flour, salt, three teaspoons Horsford's baking powder Flavor to taste. Fry in lard.

DOUGHNUTS.

Mrs. Lovejoy.

One quart milk, one and one-half pound sugar, one pound butter, four eggs, one nutmeg, one cup yeast. Set the sponge with the milk and butter. When light add the sugar, nutmeg and eggs, then raise again and fry.

GINGERSNAPS.

One coffee cup New Orleans molasses, one cup butter, one cup sugar; place them on the stove and let it come to a boil. Then take off immediately, and add teaspoon of soda, and a teaspoon of ginger. Roll thin and bake quickly.

JUMBLES.

Mrs. H. L. Hammond.

One-half pound butter, one-half pound sugar, half a nutmeg; then quarter of a pound flour and two eggs. Roll thin and bake.

LADY FINGERS.

Four ounces of sugar, four yolks of eggs, mix well; three ounces of flour, a little salt. Beat the four whites to a stiff froth, stir the whites into the mixture, a little at a time until all is in. Butter a shallow pan. Squirt through a confectioner's syringe or a little piece of paper rolled up. Dust with sugar and bake in a not too hot oven.

MACCAROONS.

One-half pound almonds, blanched; pound fine with one tablespoon of lemon extract (Colton's), one pound of powdered sugar, whites of three eggs. Roll out, cut in small rounds and bake on a buttered paper on a thin board.

MOLASSES COOKIES.

One pint of molasses, one-half pint of lard and butter mixed. Boil these; add one teaspoon of soda, one tablespoon of extract of lemon. When cold add flour and roll thin.

YANKEE PUFFS.

Two ounces of butter, three tablespoons of sugar, three eggs (whites and yolks separate), three teacups of milk, three teacups of flour, one saltspoon of salt, one teaspoon of vanilla. Beat the butter to a cream, add the sugar and well-beaten yolks, then the milk, which should be salted, dredge in the flour by degrees, and when these are well mixed add the flavoring and whites of eggs, previously beaten to a stiff froth. Bake in well-buttered teacups, about fifteen or twenty minutes, till of a light brown. As these puffs rise very much, the cups must not be filled. Serve as soon as done with sweet sauce.

CHOCOLATE FROSTING FOR CAKES.

One and one-half pounds of sugar, half a pint of milk, a piece of butter the size of a nutmeg, two tablespoons of plain chocolate, scraped and mixed to a paste with boiling water. Boil the sugar, milk and butter seven minutes, then place in a bowl, add the chocolate paste, stir until the mixture becomes thick, then spread; should it become too hard to spread smoothly stir in a little boiling water. The above can be used for layer cake, and is sufficient for three layers.

ICING.

Two and one-half cups sugar, two-thirds cup water; boil together until it candies; then add the whites of three eggs, slightly beaten, stirring briskly for fifteen minutes, or until it seems perfectly smooth and white; then add the juice of one lemon. This is sufficient for one large white mountain cake of eight or nine layers, covering also top and sides.

CHOCOLATE ICING.

Take the whites of two eggs, one and one-half cups powdered sugar and six large tablespoons of chocolate.

CHOCOLATE FILLING.

Whites of three eggs, one and one-half teacups of sugar, three tablespoons grated chocolate, one teaspoon vanilla. Beat the whites of the eggs well and add the other ingredients; then beat all together and spread between the layers and on top of the cake.

ICING.

Miss K. A. Bishop.

Cook one cup of sugar with water enough to cover it until it thickens, in cold water. Stir this into the well beaten white of one egg. This is sufficient for one large cake.

ICES, BLANC MANGE, ETC.

"The full soul loatheth an honey-comb, but to the hungry soul every bitter thing is sweet."

—Proverbs 27-7.

ICE CREAM.

Georgie Hill.

One quart of cream, whites of three eggs, one coffeecup of sugar; flavor to taste; one-half cup of milk; whip the cream and beat the eggs. Freeze in a White Mountain Triple Freezer one-half hour, or more if necessary.

PEACH ICE CREAM.

Georgie Hill.

Use the above recipe with eight large peaches mashed and strained through a sieve. Put in a teacup of sugar, and add to the above recipe. Use no other flavoring but the peaches.

ITALIAN CREAM.

Rub the zest of two lemons upon three or four lumps of loaf sugar; stir these into a pint of rich cream and add enough sugar to sweeten. Whip the cream with the juice of one lemon, straining in one ounce of gelatine that has been dissolved in a little water. When thoroughly light flavor to taste and pour into a mould and freeze. When served garnish with preserved fruit.

MACCAROON GLACE.

Mrs. A. D. Smith.

Whip one quart of cream, roll one-half pound of maccaroons very fine, flavor with vanilla, sweeten to taste and freeze in a White Mountain Triple Freezer, in twenty minutes.

NESSELRODE PUDDING.

Mrs. A. D. Smith.

One-half cup of milk, two eggs, one cup granulated sugar; beat the eggs very light, put all together and boil until it becomes like cream; when cool, add one cup strong coffee, one cup cream, forty-cent box of figs chopped fine, one teaspoon burnt sugar. Freeze. This makes two quarts.

NEW YORK ICE CREAM.

Mrs. A. D. Smith.

Boil one pint of milk, stir in yolks of four eggs, beaten with one-half cup of sugar; let it get cold; one pint of cream stirred into custard, sweeten to taste, flavor with vanilla and freeze in a White Mountain Freezer. The best in the market.

ORANGE ICE.

Georgie Hill.

Five large oranges, two lemons—squeeze well. Dissolve one-half pound of sugar in a quart of water; when cool add the juice of the oranges and lemon, and freeze.

ORANGE SOUFFLE.

Georgie Hill.

The juice of four oranges, one quart of cream and the whites of three eggs, one and one-half cups of sugar and more, if necessary. Freeze as in ice cream recipes.

FAIRY BUTTER.

Beat in a mortar the yolks of four hard-boiled eggs, three ounces of fine sugar, three ounces of butter, two ounces of blanched almonds, and a tablespoon of orange-flower water. When reduced to a paste, mould and freeze it, and serve with sweet biscuits round.

SHERBET.

Mrs. H. H. Gregg.

To one quart of strong lemonade add white of one egg; use any fruit chopped fine, always using one quart water for every quart of sherbet desired, and adding the white of egg not beaten. Freeze in a White Mountain Freezer from twenty to thirty minutes.

PINEAPPLE SHERBET.

Mrs. D. Le Bettee.

One quart pineapple, one pint sugar, one pint water, two tablespoons of gelatine in half the pint of water (hot), add sugar to juice of pineapple. Freeze twenty minutes.

TUTTI FRUTTI ICE CREAM.

Mrs. A. D. Smith.

When a plain cream of any kind is partly frozen, crystalized fruit of any kind chopped fine may be added, having the same quantity of fruit as you have ice cream. Chopped citron, raisins, English currants, or any candied fruit may be used. Put into a mould and pack in ice and salt. It may be served with a whipped cream around it.

CHOCCLATE BLANC MANGE.

One quart milk, one ounce Cooper's gelatine soaked in a cup of the milk one hour, four heaping spoons grated chocolate rubbed up with a little milk, three eggs, white and yolks beaten separately, three-fourths cup sugar, two teaspoons vanilla. Heat the milk to boiling, pour in the gelatine and milk, and stir until it is dissolved, add the sugar to the beaten yolks, and stir until smooth; beat the chocolate into this, and pour in spoon by spoon the scalding milk upon the mixture, stirring all the time until all is in. Return to the inner sauce pan and heat gradually, stirring faithfully until it almost boils. Remove from the fire, turn into a bowl, and whip in briskly and lightly the beaten whites with the vanilla. Set to form in moulds wet with cold water. Eat with whipped cream.

COFFEE BLANC MANGE.

One quart of cream (part milk can be used), one-half package of gelatine, one-half cup of strong coffee, one cup of sugar. Soak the gelatine one hour in one-half cup of cold water, add the coffee hot, then the sugar. Set it on the range until the gelatine is thoroughly dissolved, then set aside until partly cold, whip the cream and pour it gradually into the mixture. Pour it into a mould and set aside to harden.

DELICIOUS BLANC MANGE.

Put an ounce of gelatine in a little warm water and keep it on the stove until dissolved, then sweeten one quart of cream, add extract of lemon or vanilla and whip it. Strain the gelatine on the cream. Wet your moulds in cold water, fill them and set them away to congeal.

GELATINE BLANC MANGE.

Mrs. D. W. Coan.

Soak one-half box gelatine in one and one-half pints of milk for one hour; put it over a kettle of boiling water, and when it comes to a boil add the beaten yolks of three eggs, and six tablespoons of sugar. Stir briskly for a few minutes. When plenty cool add the whites of the eggs beaten very light. Flavor with vanilla. Cool in a mould, and serve with sugar and cream.

GELATINE BLANC MANGE.

Mrs. C. E. Crandall.

One-half box of gelatine (Cox's), one and a half pints milk; put on kettle boiling water, and when it comes to boil add well beaten yolks of three eggs, and four tablespoons of sugar. Stir briskly for few minutes. Let partly cool, and add whites of three eggs beaten very light, flavor; pour in mould. Serve with cream and sugar. Must stand five or six hours.

NEAPOLITAN BLANC MANGE.

Mrs. J. Anderson.

One quart milk, one box gelatine (soaked one hour), one cup sugar. Heat the milk to boiling, add the gelatine and stir ten minutes before adding the sugar. Strain through a cheesecloth bag, and separate the mixture into four parts. Leave one part uncolored. Color No. 2 with a tablespoon of chocolate rubbed to a paste. No. 3 with the yolk of an egg. No. 4 with a tablespoon of currant jelly. Stir parts two and three over the fire till very hot. When quite cold, pour into a wet mould the white paste first, then the yellow, then the pink, and finally the chocolate. Set in a cool place.

VELVET BLANC MANGE.

Two cups sweet cream, one-half ounce Cooper's gelatine soaked in a very little cold water one hour, one-half cup white powdered sugar, one teaspoon extract of bitter almond, one glass of white wine. Heat the cream to boiling, stir in the gelatine and sugar, and as soon as they are dissolved take from the fire, beat ten minutes until very light, flavor and add the wine by degrees, mixing it well. Put into moulds wet with clear water.

ROMAN CREAM.

One-half box of gelatine, one-half glass of milk, three tablespoons of granulated sugar, one gill of wine, one pint of cream, whites of two eggs, vanilla to taste; soak the gelatine in the milk half an hour, then put the dish in which it has been soaked in a basin of hot water on the stove until the gelatine is entirely dissolved. Whip the cream light, add the sugar and vanilla, then the whites beaten to a stiff froth. Stir the gelatine into the cream, sugar, etc., slowly and beat it well. Pour it into a mould and set it on the ice to harden.

SNOW CREAM.

One-half box of gelatine, the whites of three eggs, a teacup of white sugar. Flavor with extract of vanilla. Beat the whites of the eggs to a stiff froth; pour a pint of boiling water on the gelatine. Let it cool, but do not let it get stiff. Beat it into the eggs and sugar.

SPANISH CREAM.

Mrs. W. A. Hammond.

One quart milk, one cup sugar, one package gelatine, one-half teaspoon salt, one teaspoon vanilla, yolks of four eggs. Beat eggs to a froth. Heat milk and stir in other ingredients. Use whites for meringues or cake.

WHIPPED CREAM.

One pint of sweet cream, sweetened to taste; one teaspoon of vanilla. Put the cream in a bowl and beat with a wheel egg-beater until thick, then sweeten and flavor. The cream will beat better if cold (the whites of two eggs beaten to a stiff froth may be added).

Different jellies or fruits may be served with it. This is a delicious dessert.

CHARLOTTE RUSSE.

Mrs. J. Anderson.

Two dozen lady-fingers, one quart rich cream, one cup powdered sugar, two teaspoons vanilla extract. Split the cakes and fit nicely around the sides of a deep dish or small glasses; sweeten and flavor the cream, beat to a stiff froth; pour the mixture into the dish and set upon the ice to cool. Or take a sponge cake, cut the top evenly off, scoop out the middle of the cake very carefully, wet the inside crust with wine, pour in the mixture and replace the top.

PALACE BUFFET SLEEPING CARS

.... RUN DAILY BETWEEN ....

CHICAGO AND NASHVILLE,

THIS ROUTE IS THE MOST DIRECT ONE TO OR FROM

Chattanooga, Atlanta, Macon, Savannah,
Charleston, Birmingham, Montgomery,
And All Points in FLORIDA, and is the Scenic Route

TO OR FROM

MOBILE and NEW ORLEANS

For Rates, Time Table and information in detail, address
any Coupon Ticket Agent in the North or South.

Chicago City Ticket Office, 64 Clark Street,
(Sherman House.)

F. E. SCOTT, City Pass. and Ticket Agent, CHICAGO, ILL.
WILLIAM HILL, General Pass. and Ticket Agent,
Chicago & Eastern Illinois R. R.

CHARLOTTE RUSSE.

Mrs. Dr. Leroy.

N. B.—The cake must be one day old.

Cake: Four eggs, one cup sugar, one cup flour, pinch of salt; flavor with vanilla. Filling: Five eggs, one-half coffee cup sugar, tablespoon of vanilla, one-half package of gelatine (Coxe). two-thirds cup of milk, one-half cup of very thick cream made cold on the ice. Soak the gelatine in half of the milk. Beat the yolks of the eggs and sugar together, and put in double boiler with the remaining milk. Stir until the mixture begins to thicken, then add the gelatine; when cold add the whites of eggs well beaten. Whip the cream and mix with the flavoring all together, and pour into a mould lined with cake. Elegant.

CHARLOTTE RUSSE.

Mary S. Shelton.

Select a pan or mould the size you wish to line, then bake sponge cake in thin cakes, the sizes according to your mould; also bake a thin cake large enough to cover the top. Whip a quart of thick cream; put an ounce of Coxe's gelatine in a pint of warm milk, and set on the back of the stove until dissolved, then strain it. To one-half pint of pale sherry wine add a cup of sugar and a teaspoon of vanilla; add this to the gelatine. When almost cold, but not congealed, pour this into the whipped cream, stir well and sweeten mo.e if desired. Put on the cover of cake and let it stand in a cold place till firm, then turn out and cover with a thin frosting.

BAKED MILK FOR INVALIDS.

Put two quarts of fresh milk into a jar and bake eight or ten hours. When done sufficiently it will be as thick as cream, and can be eaten by very delicate persons.

FRUIT JELLIES, PRESERVES.

APPLE JELLY.

Cut two pounds of sweet apples into quarters, without peeling, throwing them into cold water as you cut them. Then put them into a preserving-pan, with a quart of fresh, cold water, and boil until they become a pulp, adding as the apple boils one pound of loaf sugar, and a little vanilla. Then run it through a jelly bag; it must stand some hours to allow it to pass through completely. It must then be simmered over the fire twenty minutes, to jelly, and poured into the mould.

APPLE OR PEAR JELLY.

Pare and quarter ripe, juicy apples or pears, and boil them at a great distance from the fire till they become a jam. Have ready a rich syrup, and add in proportion of one pint of syrup to three pounds of fruit, and boil for a quarter of an hour. Turn out into pots.

APPLE COMPOTE.

Mrs. Willis Blackman.

Take one quart of water and one pint of sugar, six tart apples, core and pare them and stew in syrup until tender. Take out without breaking and lay them in a glass dish. Add a box of gelatine and three or four sticks of cinnamon to the syrup when thoroughly dissolved, pour over the apples.

COMPOTE OF APPLES.

Compotes of fruits of all kinds are either used for *entremets* garnished with biscuits or pastry, or for dessert. They are usually served in deep glass dishes, known in the dessert service as *compotiers*. Pare a pound of golden pippins or any good apples, and core without breaking them; make a syrup of ten ounces of loaf sugar, with half a pint of water; let it boil ten minutes to thicken; put in the apples and simmer them for twenty minutes, or till soft without being broken; then turn it out into the *compotier* to grow cool, with the syrup round.

COMPOTE OF PEARS.

Make a syrup of ten ounces of sugar, half a pint of water, and two cloves; when boiled thick take out the cloves, and add a glass of port wine; put one pound of good baking pears on the fire for a few minutes in boiling water till you can draw off the skin; core them and put into the syrup; boil gently for twenty minutes, or, if the pears be large, half an hour, till they are tender; then turn out with the syrup.

BLACKBERRY JAM.

The berries are ripe and plentiful in September, and merely require nice picking, half the weight of any kind of sugar, and three-quarters of an hour boiling. The single objection to the jam is the quantity of seeds; but the jelly made from this fruit is perfect.

CRANBERRY JELLY.

Dissolve one ounce of isinglass in three-quarters of a pint of water; then draw out over the fire and press the cranberries, and add the isinglass jelly to a pint and a half of the juice, a dessert-spoon of lemon juice, six ounces of sugar, and the whites and crushed shells of four eggs. Simmer ten minutes; then strain through muslin till clear, and fill the mould.

POTTED PEARS.

Take ripe pears, wipe them carefully; place a layer, stem upwards, in a stone jar, sprinkle over sugar, then set in another layer of pears, more sugar, and so on, until the jar is filled. To every gallon put in a pint and a half of water. Cover the jar close, and set in a slow oven two hours. It is a nice dish for the tea table, with or without cream.

GORDON & DILWORTH

MANUFACTURING PURVEYORS

ESTABLISHED 1847.

ALL OF OUR PRODUCTIONS BEAR THIS TRADE MARK. WILL PROSECUTE ALL IMITATIONS & INFRINGEMENTS OF THE SAME

OVER 100 DOMESTIC & FOREIGN FRUITS & VEGETABLES TRANSMUTED INTO TABLE DELICACIES

PRICES ON PRESERVES REDUCED DEC. 1ST. 1885.

OUR PRESERVES & JELLIES

HAVE LED THE MARKET FOR 40 YEARS

OUR MINCE MEAT & PLUM PUDDING

ARE SIMPLY INCOMPARABLE.

OUR SALAD DRESSING & NEW PROCESS CATSUP

GIVE TONE TO THE MOST MODEST REPAST,

WHILE OUR

OLIVES CAPERS AND BRANDY FRUITS

ADDED THERETO, TRANSFORM IT INTO A FEAST.

FOR SALE BY THE LEADING GROCERS ON THE AMERICAN CONTINENT.

SEE OTHER SIDE

GORDON & DILWORTH

MANUFACTURING PURVEYORS

ESTABLISHED 1847.

SEE OTHER SIDE.

ORANGE JAM.

Weigh the oranges before peeling, and put a pound of sugar to a pound of fruit. Take the peel from half the oranges, grate it, and add the sugar. Open the oranges, and be very particular to get out the seeds and white strings. Add to the sugar and peel, with a little water, and boil twenty minutes.

RASPBERRY, CURRANT, OR GOOSEBERRY JAM.

These jams all require three-quarters of their weight in sugar; but the fruit must be boiled first till broken. The raspberries and currants will not require more than half an hours previous boiling, the gooseberries nearly an hour, before the sugar is added, when they must boil twenty-five to thirty minutes more. Be careful to stir, and to remove the scum. Gooseberry jam is much improved by the addition of a small quantity of red or black currant juice.

BRANDIED CHERRIES.

Mrs. J. Anderson.

Make a syrup of one pound sugar, and one wine glass water to two pounds fruit. Heat to boiling, stirring to prevent burning, pour over the cherries, and let stand fully one hour. Then put all into the preserving kettle, *heat slowly* and boil five minutes. Take out the fruit with a perforated skimmer and fill the bottle two-thirds full. Boil the syrup twenty minutes, adding one pint best brandy to five pounds fruit, pour over the cherries scalding hot and seal.

BRANDY PEACHES.

Mrs. H. H. Brown.

Pare the peaches after rubbing the outside off—an easy way is to put them in boiling water when the skin comes off with rubbing. Boil in water enough to cover them until clear and tender, then place on a platter, weigh, and to one pound of fruit use one pound of granulated sugar, using the water the peaches were boiled in for the syrup. When sufficiently boiled to become thick, drop the peaches in one by one lest they break; let them cook a little when done. The same recipe will do for plums and pears.

PICKLED PEACHES OR PEARS.

Mrs. J. Anderson.

Prick the fruit with a fork to prevent bursting and stick a few whole cloves in each peach or pear. Heat in just enough water to cover them, then remove the fruit and add to the water three and one-half pounds sugar to seven pounds fruit. Boil twenty minutes, add two quarts cider vinegar (or three pints vinegar and one pint water), one tablespoon allspice, one tablespoon mace tied in a bag, some stick cinnamon, and whole cloves, and boil together ten minutes. Drop in the fruit a few at a time and boil until they can be pierced with a straw. Take out the fruit, pack in glass jars or air-tight crocks, boil the syrup until thick and pour over the fruit scalding hot.

PICKLED WATERMELON OR CITRON RIND.

Mrs. J. Anderson.

Cut the rind into narrow strips or fancy cuttings and lay in brine for a few days, then steam over a clear fire until the rinds are clear and soft. Prepare a syrup, allowing same quantity of sugar as you have rind, one cup water to one pound sugar, and one-half ounce root ginger (tied in a bag). When the syrup is *almost* boiling drop in the rinds and simmer until they are perfectly clear. Then take them out, add to the syrup one pint cider vinegar to one pound sugar, and mace, cloves, and cinnamon to taste. Boil up once, throw in some stick cinnamon and whole cloves, and pour over the rinds scalding hot. Keep in stone crocks with perfectly fitting covers.

PICKLED RAISINS.

Mrs. H. H. Brown.

Two cups of vinegar well spiced with cinnamon and cloves, one and a third cups of sugar, set it on the fire, have ready bunches of table raisins, and when hot put them in. This makes a handsome dish for the table. The syrup must boil and the raisins left until they swell and look full like grapes.

PRESERVED PEACHES.

Twelve pounds of large peaches, eight pounds of sugar, one pint of vinegar; pare and steam fruit till tender, steaming a few at a time. Put vinegar and sugar together, when boiling put in the steamed peaches and let them boil up. Take the peaches out with a skimmer.

STRAWBERRIES PRESERVED WHOLE.

Take equal weights of strawberries and loaf sugar, put the sugar into a pan with merely sufficient water to dissolve it, and let it boil till the surface is covered with small bubbles; this will probably be in about twenty minutes; then put the fruit, with one pint of red currant juice to each pound of strawberries, which improves the color. Allow it to boil five minutes, then put into small jars. It is not necessary to use more sugar for the currant juice, the strawberries being of themselves so sweet. Red currants or raspberries, with the addition of white currant juice, black currant, apricot or other jams, may be made in this way.

SPICED CITRON.

Prepare the fruit, cover with vinegar and let it stand over night, in the morning pour off, and to every seven pounds of fruit allow three and one-half pounds of white sugar and a pint of vinegar; tie in a muslin bag a tablespoon of each of the different spices; make a syrup of the sugar, put in the fruit and cook for one-half hour. When all the fruit is done, add the vinegar, and let the sypup boil thick, pour it over the fruit, and let it get cold before sealing up the jars.

SPICED CURRANTS.

Make a syrup of three pounds of sugar, one pint of vinegar, two tablespoons of cinnamon, two tablespoons of cloves, and half a teaspoon of salt. Add six pounds of currants, and boil half an hour.

SPICED GOOSEBERRIES.

Mrs. Hammond.

To one pound of gooseberries take three quarters of a pound of sugar, and one pint of vinegar to ten pints of this mixture when boiling. No water; cinnamon, allspice, cloves, and nutmeg to taste. Let it cook three or four hours.

SPICED PLUMS.

Seven quarts of plums, three and one-half pounds sugar, one ounce ground cloves, one ounce cinnamon, one quart vinegar. Boil one-half hour.

BAKED QUINCES.

The quince eaten hot, with either cream or a dot of butter on top, is a revelation to most people. The quince should be well sprinkled with sugar before putting the dish in the oven. Neither core nor pare them, as the baked seeds add to their jelly richness. They are highly esteemed for dessert.

QUINCE JELLY.

Cover the fruit with water and boil until the goodness is all out (it will require one-half or three-fourths of an hour). Then strain through flannel or crash,without much squeezing. Strain twice if not clear; add equal quantities of juice and sugar, and boil steadily about twenty minutes. It is better to leave the glasses several days before sealing, even if not quite hard, as your jelly will be much more delicate than if boiled too long.

QUINCE JELLY.

Wash the fruit, save all the nice parings and seeds; cook for an hour or more in more water than will cover them, then run them through the colander and let them stand until next day, or until the fruit substance has settled: now throw off the clear juice through a thin muslin bag and place on the fire. When boiling well add one pint of sugar to each pint of juice, and boil until it rolls off the spoon; fill the jelly cups, and let them sit by the stove or any warm place a couple of days without covers, so as to evaporate any water if the jelly is not stiff enough.

Any jelly is better to be taken from the fire before quite done as it will finish by setting on the heater or near a warm stove, and if it boils one minute too long it will never be anything but a sticky, good-for-nothing kind of syrup.

Apple or any fruit jelly can be made by boiling the fruit (not skins and seeds) and treated in the same way.

To prevent mould on glasses of jelly, lay a lump of parafine on top of the hot jelly, letting melt and spread over it, or melt it first and pour over the jelly when cold.

STRAWBERRY JELLY.

Equal weight of sugar and strawberry juice. Press some ripe strawberries through a delicately clean cloth, then strain the juice very clean, and stir into it an equal weight of sugar. When the sugar is dissolved put into a double boiler over a clear fire, and let it boil for half an hour, skimming it carefully as the scum rises. Put into glass jars or pots, and when cold cover it over as above directed.

RHUBARB AND ORANGE PRESERVES.

Six oranges, two pounds of rhubarb stalks, one pound and a half of sugar. Peel the oranges carefully, take away the white rind and pulps, slice the pulps into a double boiler with the peel cut very small, add the rhubarb cut very fine, and sugar. Boil the whole down in the usual way for preserves.

PUNCH JELLY.

One pint cold water, one pint boiling water, one box Cox's gelatine, one wine glass wine, one wine glass brandy, juice of two lemons, one pound granulated sugar. Soak the gelatine in the cold water one hour; add the boiling water, the lemon juice, the sugar, and stir till the gelatine is dissolved. Strain, add the wine and brandy, and pour into a mould.

BEVERAGES.

Note:—In making tea, coffee or chocolate, always see that the water in the kettle is *freshly boiled*; never use water that has been standing.

TEA.

Pour boiling water into the teapot, and let stand till it is heated through; pour off the water, add the tea, allowing one teaspoon of tea to each cup water, pour over it the boiling water and serve in five minutes.

"For making good tea and coffee use the Automatic Tea and Coffee Cooker."

COFFEE.

Three pints boiling water, one cup freshly ground coffee, one egg. Mix the egg and dry coffee together, pour the boiling water over it, boil three minutes and strain through flannel.

If the French coffee pot is used put the coffee into the top-most compartment, pour the water over it, and serve when the water has passed through the treble set of strainers.

CHOCOLATE.

One pint boiling water, one pint milk or cream, one teacup Baker's chocolate rubbed to a paste, stir the chocolate into the water and boil twenty minutes, add the milk and boil ten minutes longer, stirring frequently. Sweeten to taste.

BLACKBERRY CORDIAL.

To one peck of berries well mashed, add one ounce of cinnamon, one ounce cloves, one ounce allspice, and one nutmeg, all ground, mix and boil slowly half an hour, then strain, and to each pint of juice add one-half pound loaf sugar. Boil half an hour longer, when cool, add one quart best brandy and seal.

GINGER WINE.

Mrs. Evans.

Take five gallons of water, fifteen pounds white sugar, ten ounces of ginger, the rind of six lemons pealed very thin. Boil one hour, let it stand until evening, then put into a cask with the juice of the lemons, four pounds raisins chopped, four spoons yeast. Stir once every day, then add one-half ounce of isinglass, and one pint of brandy. Stop it close, and in three months it will be fit to bottle.

GRAPE WINE.

Mrs. H. H. Brown.

Put one gallon of water to one gallon of bruised grapes. Let it stand one week without stirring, then drain off the liquor, and to each gallon of straining add three pounds of sugar. Put in a barrel or cask loosly corked until fermented, then cork tightly for two months, when it will be clear and ready to bottle. Must be kept in a dry cellar. Care must be taken in pulling the fruit to save the juice. Put into jars. Let the syrup cool, then stir in the Brandy, mixing thoroughly, then pour over the fruit. To half a peck of grapes use a quart of the best brandy.

RHUBARB WINE.

To every gallon of water add five pounds ot ripe rhubarb cut in thin slices as for preserves. Let it stand nine days, frequently stirring it, and keeping the cask covered to exclude the air. Strain and squeeze through a coarse cloth or flannel

strainer. To every gallon of liquor add four pounds lump sugar, the juice of two lemons and rind of one.—To clear it, dissolve one ounce of isinglass in a pint of the wine and let it be quite cold before pouring into the wine; that quantity of isinglass is sufficient for nine gallons. When fermentation is over close tightly. In three months it will be fit for use.

SHRUB.

Mrs. H. Gregg.

Five quarts raspberries, one quart vinegar, two teaspoons tartaric acid. Cover raspberries over night, press through jelly bag carefully. To one quart juice add one pound sugar, scald, skim and bottle. Keep in dark place.

STRAWBERRY SHERBET.

One quart strawberries, three pints water, juice of two lemons, one pound white sugar. Crush the berries, add water and lemon juice, and let stand three hours. Strain *over* the sugar (squeezing hard), and stir till sugar is dissolved. Strain again and set on ice two hours before using it.

The Haymarket,

WEST MADISON AND HALSTED STS.

A Thoroughly First-Class Family Theatre and the Most Elegant, Roomy and Comfortable Place of Amusement in Chicago.

Popular Prices Always and the Best Attractions.

WILL J. DAVIS, MANAGER.

CANDY.

A new receipt is given for making nut candy, that has been tested. To two cups of granulated sugar and one of boiling water, add one large tablespoon of butter. Boil till it readily candies when dropped in cold water. Then remove from the fire and stir in nearly two cups of Brazil nuts, cut up small, and one tablespoon of lemon flavoring. Pour out upon four large buttered plates to cool. Always use a silver spoon in stirring candy. Home-made candy is a very desirable adjunct to the dessert, and consoles the children when deprived of the pastrys or puddings that prove so attractive to them.

SUGARED ALMONDS.

Make a syrup of one pint of water to a pound of sugar, and when boiling, stir in blanched Jordan almonds for ten minutes; take them out, and dry, and reduce the syrup one-half; then dip the almonds in again for a minute, and with the thick syrup adhering to them, dry them on an inverted sieve in a warm place, and store in a tin box.

CHOCOLATE CREAM CANDY.

Georgie Hill.

Three cups sugar, one-half cup water, one-half tablespoon of vinegar, one-half of a hen's egg of butter, one teaspoon of vanilla, one square of Baker's chocolate, grated; stir all together, then put on the stove, try it in a cup of cold water; when done put on buttered tins; cut in squares when cold enough. Do not stir while on the stove.

MOLASSES CANDY.

One quart of New Orleans molasses, two pounds brown sugar; boil from an hour and a half to two hours. No butter for hands necessary.

MOLASSES CREAM CANDY.

Miss A. K. Boyden.

Two cups molasses, one small cup sugar, one tablespoon vinegar, butter size of a walnut; boil until it hardens when dropped into cold water, and then pour in a cup of cream. Let the mixture continue cooking until it becomes brittle, when again try in water. While cooking stir constantly, and when done pour in buttered pans; cool and pull.

OPERA CREAM CARAMELS.

Two cups of granulated sugar, one cup of milk, two even tablespoons of butter, one teaspoon of vanilla; boil the sugar and milk together for ten minutes, then add the butter and flavoring, and boil until it will grain.

BRAZIL NUT CANDY.

Two pounds of confectioner's sugar, half a cup of milk, half a cup of water, butter the size of a walnut: boil together until the candy will grain, then add one pound before cracking of Brazil nuts sliced in fine pieces, and stir until well grained, then add a teaspoonful of .vanilla, cool it a little, and cut in squares.

HICKORY NUT CANDY.

Two cups golden syrup, one cup sugar, one tablespoon of vinegar, small piece of butter—about one-half tablespoon; boil about twenty minutes or until it hardens slightly when dropped in water; prepare hickory, pecan or almond nuts together or separately, spread on a large buttered platter, and pour candy over them; cut in squares when partly cold.

VANILLA CREAM CANDY.

Georgie Hill.

Three cups sugar, one-half cup water, one tablespoon of vinegar, one-half of a large hen's egg of butter, one teaspoon vanilla: stir all together before placing on the stove, then don't stir; take off when done (can tell by testing in a cup of water), and pour on buttered plates; pull when cool. Delicious.

POP CORN BALLS.

Put the popcorn on a platter and pour over it the vanilla cream candy before quite done, and make into balls before it is cool.

FRENCH CREAM CANDY.

Take two cups of granulated sugar, one of cold water, one and one-half tablespoons arrowroot, dissolve this in cold water and pour on sugar; boil fron ten to twenty minutes, stirring all the time; boil until the syrup thickens and drops heavily from the spoon, then take from the fire and put the pan into cold water, beating the contents to a smooth, white cream. Before it is cool add a tablespoon of vanilla, take the cream, a little at a time, and mould into any desired shape. It should be about the consistency of putty, and work easily. If it is dry and crumbles it is cooked too much, and you must add a little water and boil again. When the cream is moulded take a cake of Baker's chocolate, scrape fine, put into a bowl, set this in a kettle of boiling water until the chocolate is melted, then add two tablespoons pulverized sugar, and beat until smooth. Into this drop the cream balls, one at a time; take out and place on buttered paper until cold.

BUTTER SCOTCH.

Seven tablespoons molasses, two tablespoons of water, two tablespoons of sugar, two tablespoons of butter. Boil until it will work easily when dropped in cold water.

BUTTER SCOTCH.

One cup of brown sugar, one-half cup of water, one teaspoon of vinegar, piece of butter size of a walnut. Boil about twenty minutes. Flavor if desired.

MISCELLANEOUS RECIPES.

CLEANSING CREAM.

Mrs. H. H. Brown.

Four ounces castile soap, four ounces aqua ammonia, one ounce sulphuric ether, one ounce alcohol. Cut the soap fine, dissolve in one quart of water; add the ingredients; lastly five quarts of soft water. If you wish to remove spots, rub a little on with a sponge, but to clean a large surface, add a little warm water and sponge off with it. This can be used on any fabric.

POT POURRI.

Mrs. Gibbs, Rochester, N. Y.

One and a half peck rose leaves, place in a deep bowl in thin layers, with a handful of salt sprinkled on each layer. Let it remain five days, turning twice a day. This should appear moist. Add three ounces of bruised allspice, one ounce stick cinnamon crushed. This forms the stock. Allow it to remain a week, turning daily from bottom to top. Then put into permanent jars one ounce of allspice, adding the stock layer by layer. Sprinkle between the layers the following mixture: One ounce cloves, one ounce cinnamon, two nutmegs, coarsely powdered, two ounces ginger root sliced thin, half an ounce anise seed bruised, ten grains finest musk, two ounces sliced orris root, half pound dried lavender leaves. Then add the following essential oils at pleasure, some perfer one, some another: lemon, verbena, geranium, jessamine, cologne water tripple extract, or any freshly dried flowers that are fragrant. Shake and stir the jar once or twice a week. Open only during the daily odorizing. This will last a long time.

THE ECONOMICAL FRUIT PRESERVATIVE.

Take the fruit as soon after being picked as possible, see that it is sound and clean, pack tightly in a jar or crock, then pour on the following composition: Dissolve thoroughly salicylic acid thirty-five grains, sugar eight ounces, to one quart of water and one gallon of fruit.

FOR GREEN CORN.

Acid three and one-half drams, salt four ounces, one gallon of water. Always dissolve acid in hot water.

TO SWEEP CARPETS.

Wash dry and chop potatoes, spread them on one side of the room and sweep across the carpet.

TO REMOVE IRON RUST.

The juice of lemon and salt placed on the spot, and the fabric put in the sun, will remove rust. Shining through glass its rays are stronger. I hang mine in a window.

TO CLEAN ZINC.

Wet the zinc all over with muriatic acid, sprinkle over it very fine sand or ashes, then scour, wash and dry. Or rub with kerosene.

RECIPE FOR BRONZING.

Use Peerless Bronze Paints and follow directions on package.

TO TAKE SPOTS OF PAINT OFF WOOD.

Lay a thick coating of lime and soda mixed together over it, letting it stay twenty-four hours, then wash off with warm water, and the spot will have disappeared.

LAUNDRY POLISH.

One ounce gum arabic, one ounce borax to two pints of water (dissolved). Use two tablespoons to a quart of starch.

TO REMOVE FRUIT STAINS.

Place your muslin over a tub, hold it firmly, and pour hot water through the spot stained, and it will soon disappear. This must be done before putting the muslin in soapsuds.

TO POLISH FURNITURE.

Mix sufficient vinegar in linseed oil to cut it; with this saturate raw cotton, over which place soft muslin; rub lightly over the article.

To wash silk handkerchiefs soak them first in cold salt water for ten minutes, or longer, then wash out in the same water and iron it immediately. Carpets may be greatly brightened by first sweeping thoroughly and then going over them with a clean cloth and clear salt and water. Use a cup of coarse salt to a basin of water. Salt in the whitewash will make it stick better. Wash the mica of the stove doors with salt and vinegar. Brass work can be kept beautifully bright by occasionally rubbing with salt and vinegar. To clean willow furniture use salt and water. Apply it with a nail brush, scrub well and dry thoroughly.

TO PREVENT JARS BREAKING.

When putting in the fruit set the cold jar on a folded cloth wet with cold water; then fill with the boiling hot fruit. I have never known a jar to break when thus treated.

Cold biscuits left over from tea may be made better than when first baked by dipping them into hot water and placing them singly on the hot grate in the oven long enough to let them get well warmed through.

Remove the cover from the pot after pouring off the water from boiled potatoes and leave them on the back part of the stove, thus allowing the steam to escape. This will leave them mealy.

Vinegar is better than ice for keeping fish. By putting a little vinegar on the fish it will keep perfectly well even in hot weather. Fish is often improved in flavor under this treatment.

A small bag of sulphur kept in a drawer or closet that is infested with red ants will quickly disperse them.

TO DESTROY COCKROACHES.

Mrs. E. J. H.

I have been successful in driving away, if not exterminating, cockroaches by scattering powdered borax in their haunts.

Chinese gloss starch is made of two tablespoons of raw starch, one tablespoon of borax, dissolved in one and one-half cups of cold water. Dip the thoroughly dry unstarched cuffs, collars and bosoms of shirts in this, then roll them up tight and let them remain a few hours in a a dry cloth, then rub off and iron.

Ink stains may be removed from white goods by saturating the spot with water and then covering with pounded salts of lemon. Put in the sun for five minutes, wash with soap and rinse. A paste of chloride of lime and water well rubbed in will take ink stains from silver and plated ware. Wash and wipe as usual.

Stains from tea or coffee will come out at once if they be taken immediately and held over a pail while boiling water is turned over them.

Put tea and coffee away in air-tight receptacles as soon as they are brought to the house. They lose much of their flavor by standing uncovered.

FRUIT STAINS.

To remove fruit stains from hands, wash in clear water, dry slightly, and hold hand to the flames of a lighted match.

FOR BURNS.

Use a paste made of baking soda and water.

FOR SORES.

One part carbolic acid, ten parts glycerine, forms a preparation for healing sores quickly.

DRY CLEANING.

Clean all flannels, knit and crocheted yarns with flour. Rub the articles in a pan of flour until clean, and shake thoroughly.

FOR CLEANING CARPETS AND WOOL GOODS.

One bar white ivory soap cut in fine shavings and boil in one gallon of hot water until dissolved; then add four ounces of borax, eight ounces of salsoda, stir until melted: four ounces of Fuller's earth; stir in slowly nine gallons of cold water, one-half pint alcohol.

RENOVATING FURS.

Take a large tin pan, put a pint of wheat flour in it, put the cloak in it, rub in thoroughly witn the hands until the flour looks dark; then if the fur is not white enough, rub it again with more clean flour; then rub it with pulverized chalk—5 cents worth is enough. This gives it a pearly-white look. It is also good to clean knit nubias.

SOAP FOR FLANNELS.

Two gallons of water, six bars of soap, one pint of ammonia, one of turpentine.

TO CLEAN THE INSIDE OF A TEA POT.

If the inside of your tea or coffee pot is black from long use, fill it with water, throw in a piece of hard soap; set upon the stove and let it boil from half an hour to an hour. It will clean as bright as a new dollar, and cost no work.

SOAP.

Mrs. Graham.

One box or ball of Babbitts' potash, four pounds of grease, two gallons of water. Put the potash in water, and when dissolved put in the grease, and boil four or five hours in an iron boiler; then throw in a small handful of salt, and pour into a washtub to cool. Then cut in any shape you care to.

TOILET SOAP.

The folowing soap is quite as good as any sold, and costs but little: Take two ounces of glycerine, an ounce of oil of sweet almonds, two ounces of florentine orris root, and melt with four ounces of mutton tallow, and a pound of English white castile soap. Before the soap sets it can be cut with a knife in any shape the fancy dictates. There is no soap superior to it, as a trial will prove.

DIRECTIONS FOR DYEING OVER OTHER COLORS.

Most goods to be colored are dyed over other colors. It is desirable to discharge as much of the old color as possible. This may be very well done by boiling in strong soapsuds and rinsing as long as any color is discharged. In all cases goods must be clean or dye will not take evenly. And it is best to wash well with soap, soda or borax. Rinse perfectly in clean water, then dye. For colors on cotton use stronger liquors than the same dye on wool. For fine colors follow directions on packages of PEERLESS DYES very carefully, and do not use an iron or old tin vessel.

The cheapest and best way to black stockings, that will neither fade nor color the skin or clothing, is to buy them white or light colors of either silk, wool or cotton, and dye them with Peerless Dye. No other colors will stand the washing that stockings get.

TAR WATER CURE FOR FALLING HAIR.

I am a woman possessed with a little more than the allotted share of the crowning glory given to my sex, and when my beauty was seized with a freak to fall out and leave me, it is not surprising that I became alarmed. After trying everything (with no success), I chanced to see the tar water remedy prescribed in *The Home.* Prepared the water according to directions, used it faithfully, and now my head is covered with a soft down of new hair. I did not apply the tar to the scalp, however. I applied it to the water thusly: To a pint of boiling soft water, two tablespoons of the tar; after stirring thoroughly set away to cool; when ready strain through a thin cloth into a bottle, and the tar water is ready for use.

ADVERTISEMENTS.

INDEX.

LEE'S DRUG STORES,

COR. HALSTED and HARRISON STREETS,
COR. VAN BUREN and LAFLIN STREETS.

——ESTABLISHED A. D. 1866.——

For the compounding of Physicians' and Surgeons' Prescriptions and the sale of

Genuine Drugs and Medicines.

Drugs, Medicines and Medical Appliances retailed at Wholsale Prices.

USE MERRICK'S SPOOL COTTON

—IT IS—

SIX CORD, SOFT FINISH, FULL MEASURE,

and is equally well adapted for MACHINE or HAND SEWING.

Merrick's Spool Cotton is acknowledged by the largest consumers of thread in this country to be SUPERIOR to all others, and if you will favor us with a test of the same we are confident you will use no other.

Merrick's Ready-Wound Bobbins for Sewing Machines.

The latter are put up in packages of 200 yards each, as shown in cut. By their use TIME and LABOR are SAVED, and a more perfect stitch obtained. These Bobbins are put up for all the standard machines, and are for sale by leading dry goods houses and sewing machine agencies.

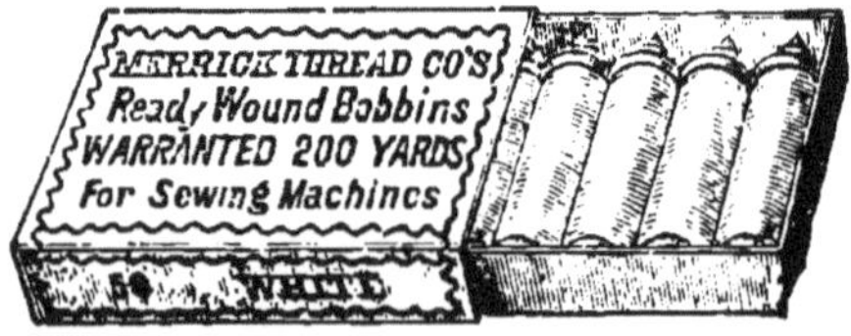

General Western Agency, 205 Fifth Avenue, Chicago.

www.ingramcontent.com/pod-product-compliance
Lightning Source LLC
Chambersburg PA
CBHW030311270326
41926CB00010B/1326